CHAOS - THROUGH T

TO THE BRINK AND BACK

By Deborah Ann Goode

Copyright and disclaimer @2025 by Deborah Goode

The right of Deborah Goode to be identified as the author of this work has been assigned to her in accordance with the Copyright Designs and Patents Act 1988. All rights reserved. No part of this publication may be reproduced, stored in or introduced into a retrieval system, or transmitted, in any form, or by any means (electronic, mechanical, photocopying, recording or otherwise) without the prior permission of the author. Any person who does any unauthorised act in relation to this publication may be liable to criminal prosecution and civil claims for damages. The author of this book does not dispense medical advice as a form of treatment for emotional, or medical advice without the advice and guidance from an appropriate physician, either directly or indirectly. The intent of the author is to give honest insight into severe mental health crises and give hope to your life. In the event you use any of the information in this book for yourself, the author and the publisher assume no responsibility for your actions.

DEDICATION

To my wonderful husband, daughters, parents and brothers who love me endlessly.
My G.P Practise who always prioritised my calls and gave me an appointment when I needed one.
My wonderful friends who I am blessed to have by my side everyday.
To Mike, my guide and proofreader.
And to my wonderful friend George.

FOREWARD

Good luck if you are troubled, stay safe always. Be patient with yourself and those around you, one day you will be well again.

PREFACE

I thank my husband for our partnership of thirty nine years; he has never given up on me despite the illness and the extensive pressure it caused on us both.

Thanks to the unique, loving, and good people who are my Mam and Papa. I have always and always will love you.

Thanks to my brothers for all you gave me in my life and for protecting me and allowing me to be the only daughter; sweet.

To my true friends, Thank you. You know who you are because we have embraced you on many occasions and I have thanked you sincerely for your support. Thank you for keeping in touch through good days and bad and not being offended by my swearing, lack of manners, yawning and my unstable emotions including the anger that I exhibited on many occasions through our conversations. Thank you for thinking of my words when I could not. You give love a new meaning; I love you.

A severe mental illness often has a devastating effect on the sufferer as well as the family and friends but I loved, I laughed, I was laughed at and I was dismissed.

Most people don't think you can laugh when you have depression; but you can and now I actually believe you can heal – or can you?

TABLE OF CONTENTS

Copyright & disclaimer
Dedication
Foreward
Preface
Table of contents
Empty Soul, Weary heart - poem by D.Goode

PART ONE

Chapter 1 - In The Beginning	5
Chapter 2 - Run Deb Run	16
Chapter 3 - My Work	27
Chapter 4 - The Newsflash	32
Chapter 5 - The Aftermath	38
Chapter 6 - My Illness	43
Chapter 7 - The Path of Destruction	50
Chapter 8 - Help Me!	57
Chapter 9 - My Family	65
Chapter 10 - To The Brink	74

PART TWO

Chapter 11 - The Fight With The Black Dog	78
Chapter 12 - My Brother	81
Chapter 13 - Making Progress	86
Chapter 14 - Fight or Flight	95
Chapter 15 - Friendships	106
Chapter 16 - Far Away From Home	114
Chapter 17 - The Children	118
Poem - Love by D.Goode	124

PART THREE

Chapter 18 - Listen To Me   126
Chapter 19 - Court   134
Chapter 20 - Moving on   140
Chapter 21 - The Trip   147
Chapter 22 - Dad   151
Chapter 23 - These Days   158
Chapter 24 - Are We There Yet ?   162
Chapter 25 - Self Help & Service To Others   171
Chapter 26 - Beauty and Beast   175

EMPTY SOUL, WEARY HEART

The love of my innocent children
Their love makes me get up again
Their unique eyes, smiles and scent of their skin

Any empty soul, a weary heart
I look around, I look within
Silence, I feel I have gone
I must not go, I will stay
I will teach them love
I won't break their hearts
I will guide their tender souls to be strong

Slowly into the unknown I wander
How it unfolds no one knows
Sometimes, mostly I know I'll be present
One day, I hope I'll even enjoy being there.

CHAOS – THROUGH TRAUMA

TO THE BRINK AND BACK

INTRODUCTION

A recent illness of over twelve years may be ending. I now recall my situation as post traumatic stress disorder which progressed to severe depressive episodes or vise versa as I'm unsure which came first. That simple description will do for now.

I have written this in the thought that I may help someone with depression or post traumatic stress disorder. Or someone suffering a mental health crisis and give hope to them as I write a real and honest account of what happened to me. When I first became ill, I read a lot about depression in order to gain an understanding of what was happening to me. This is when my idea of writing about my journey came to me. Initially, I believed that it could possibly help me by simply expressing my jumbled thoughts and also that it was something to 'do' in my empty days. I hope that writing it will bring clarity to myself as I try to comprehend such a confusing and debilitating illness.

It was short of a miracle that I was able to write my thoughts as a book during the illness due to the chaotic working of my brain. My memory was often substandard. Confusion and sensory overload was apparent too.

It was only in retrospect that I realised writing had been very cathartic. I also hoped in writing my whole story that I may help at least one person be empowered to keep going with their mental health issues. Or to show someone that reaching out for help is a strength; or for someone to see a future from their own despair. Even if my account brings hope to one person; the time and effort it has taken to write this will have been worth it. I certainly don't want sympathy but to explain why I am like I am and have my story heard and authenticated.

It has taken an immeasurable amount of time as I was unable to type quickly at the start of this book. The amount of time I pondered and had repetitive thoughts continuously as I lay awake at night has been endless.

The World Health Organisation (2024) states 3.8% of the population experience depression at some point in their lives and I now know it's not particular who it selects.

The illness was a result of my job, some difficult circumstances that built up around my working conditions and also of tragedy. My reaction to it all was something that I didn't anticipate or predict. I was traumatised by what happened. Coupled with depression I had to fight for my life and the ability to believe in a future worth living.

The complexity of the situation built up over a couple of years. I continued to do everything that was expected of me in my job as a midwife. I worked to enhance the situations of the families I worked with and promoted good health for them and that of their children. I knew I was doing too much but I kept going from task to task, one appointment straight to the next. Wearing my professional smiling mask, hiding the heart break inside.

I asked managers for help to find solutions to make work conditions smoother. At this time I wasn't helped or moved away from the circumstances. There were so many hurdles appearing in front of me regularly causing work related stress. The challenges built up against me. Frequently systems failed when new approaches were put into practise in various areas I worked in. There were inconsistencies in the ways co-workers worked alongside me. I held the responsibility for any errors or failings in the new systems and pressure built as my community caseload rocketted and was identified as being a third over capacity. I was encouraged to continue. So I did. I continued. Not recognising any change within myself other than increasing frustration and an increase in anxiety. Continue. Continue. I should have known something would go wrong.

I never predicted the malfunction would be in my mind. It came to me as a huge shock as I'd never suffered with emotional concerns at any other time in my life other than some mild anxiety which I managed.

During the illness, I became an insomniac. I used to survive on three hours of broken sleep at night. I used to hope night time would switch my brain to standby so that I could have a rest and break from the awfulness. But it rarely did. I suffered nightmares frequently. When I did sleep I shouted out or screamed as situations played over in my head and frightened me.

It was the hardest time of my life and the longest illness I've ever suffered. Many times I thought it wasn't possible to survive it. I thought I would lose control of my mind and take a hasty action that would lead to my death. Or that I would simply expire from the physical pain, turmoil and confusion I felt daily.

CHAPTER ONE.
IN THE BEGINNING.

It wasn't always like this. I had quite a straightforward upbringing. I was the youngest of three children and only daughter of a working class family. I liked my position in the family. My parents worked hard. My father worked seven days a week sometimes and occasionally worked away from home too. My Mam was a housewife and returned to work when I started Comprehensive school aged twelve years.

I had an uncomplicated life. I had my own room.The deep pink box room. My bed just fit beneath the window and it was three steps to reach the door. Important when you dive back into bed during the night because the dark of the night spooks you after a toilet visit as a little child! I always felt loved, even from my first memories of my Mam taking me places and saying kind things, that she loved me and thought I was lovely. Dad wasn't so demonstrative but Mam says I was always sitting on his knee so perhaps I wouldn't remember as it wasn't an unusual occurrence. Depending on the situation I had a quiet side as a small child. I could occupy myself for hours in my room full of toys and books which took me to my own little, peaceful world.

Those reading this who know of me may disagree whether I was a quiet child i.e my brothers! Once I was comfortable with people I was just like any other kid; impish, chatty, energetic and content mostly. I had a big cheeky smile and laughing eyes and a beguiling manner.

I can recall a few early memories from being around three years old. I loved being bathed in the kitchen sink after my tea. My Mam would be ready with a soft, clean towel that she had warmed and placed by the draining board. She would wrap me in it and give a nice warm cuddle. I can recall watching the children playing outside through the kitchen window and wishing it wasn't my bedtime. I could hear them. The groups of noisy children. They probably included my brothers and I wished that I could have joined in.

If the central heating malfunctioned in the winter when I was around the same age, she sat me in the open cupboard that housed the insulated hot water storage tank and it was super cosy in there sitting on the shelf as we waited for it to be fixed.

I remember playing outside on long summer days and visiting my paternal Grandparents for Saturday tea. My Nana was a lovely, happy and kind soul and a wonderful baker. She made scones, cakes, brandy snaps and sandwiches. I would meet my many cousins there and play happily for hours. I can recall always being happy. If I wasn't with my family I often played alone for hours in and around my home. I would play in my room when my cousins came over and we would ride my wooden rocking horse for hours and jump on the bed and play for hours. I was sometimes with and sometimes without my brothers. There weren't many other little girls where I lived until I was older.

I was comfortable in my own company. This became a necessity during post traumatic stress disorder and depression. It's a very lonely illness, depression. You can be in a room full of people but the noise can be overwhelming and the feeling of intense anxiety where you know logically that you are present but feel very absent and lonely at the same time.

My brothers were mischievous verging on naughty when they were young. At least it seemed that way at the time. I often watched their antics from a distance without having any desire to be involved. My brothers were much more outgoing than I was. Inside I often felt quite shy and embarrassed by their antics. Inadvertently, I became involved in their activities at times. The consequence of my brothers' actions frequently ended up with what we called an 'Annie shuffle' from my mother. It was a half run/shuffle a short distance behind the boys with her arms flailing about trying to catch them. They would dodge and dart from her determined and quick moves. Briskly grabbing for them around their shoulders until the boys gathered pace and they were up the stairs and into the safety of their room. We still giggle about that now.

My younger brother 'found' wheels and planks of wood and made a go-cart when I was about ten years old. We took it to the nearby hill and he tried it out first. It looked like great fun. He said if I pulled it up the hill I could have the next go. When we got to the top of the hill he jumped on it and sped down the hill, throwing his head back laughing at me! This happened a few times as he was so convincing that I would definitely get the next turn. He continuously teased and made fun of me but I had my turn in the end. And it was well worth the wait as I sped down the hill happily. He makes me laugh so much.

When I was not quite a teenager I would play and run and practise exercises constantly. I could stand in the middle of my bedroom, and with the open door practice handstands and rest my feet on the opposing passage wall outside of my room. One day I misjudged my position and as my legs swung over my head I kicked the door frame and it really hurt my heel. Oh the pain was awful. I couldn't and didn't tell my Mam for fear of being chastised. The pain was too much to ever try that again. Perhaps I was getting too tall and should have behaved more grown up?

If Dad was home we didn't seem to behave naughtily. He worked hard and he provided for us well but he was always tired when he was home. He sat in the same armchair in front of the television…Shh! The news was always on when he came home.

Sometimes, the boys would test his patience and they would know to move quickly. From his chair he would aim his slipper. The aim was good but always wasted; the boys were fast. They would run out of the door and slam it behind themselves before retreating to their bedroom. 'Bang!' The slipper would come to a stop as it hit the back of the closed door and the house settled down again. I just didn't want to be so loud or foolhardy or to push my parent's patience (but I guess I would have at times albeit unintentionally.) They were good parents so even now I wouldn't want them to think any other way. They did their very best for us. The development of my child's mind led me to believe that I had become indestructible and wiser than those that brought me into the world. There were a few arguments as a teenager but not too many.

    The three of us loved our annual holidays and I think my parents did too. I have fond memories of them. We felt no stress as young children but I think my parents did. The camping holidays were in Scotland year after year. Camping. Before the journey we all helped with the preparations in our own ways. The back car seat of the car would be overfull with pillows and sleeping bags and the trailer full of the large, two bedroom tent, camping equipment and food. We didn't eat out when we were on holiday as it wasn't affordable. Mam was so creative making meals on the small gas hob in the pressure cooker so we had hot dinners to fuel our busy, active bodies.

Mam was always the co-pilot and map reader during our holidays. Dad was always the driver. Dad was also the protector; thrusting his left arm to block the gap between the two front seats when he braked at speed. We were three active and precious children sliding around in the back of the car on top of the pile of silky sleeping bags. There was no legal obligation for back seat belts in those days. My Dad's driving skills were good but caused great amusement to us three when the trailer would turn the opposite way to what he expected as he reversed. Repeatedly he edged forward and backwards to turn it around when he had taken a wrong turn or to park it up when we arrived at our destination. He would feel the strain and sweat would pour out of his brow as he carried out the manoeuvres.

Sometimes clothes were handed down to me from my brothers despite being a girl. There are photos of me wearing my brothers' old jeans and particularly recall a thick brown and cream patterned cardigan. I have the photographic evidence! I wasn't a one to object really. We were always clean. Monday was clothes wash day where my Mam would stand for hours sorting piles of washing into and out of the twin tub washing machine. I was fairly laid back and accepting in those days and just went along with the routines. We had special occasion clothes too. One of my favourites is a certain photograph of the family with my dad and brothers dressed in their bright purple, highly patterned shirts with large rounded collars, woolly tank tops and huge ties. My Mam and I are in our dresses ready for a special occasion. It was maybe one of my little cousins' christenings. I also have a photo of when I was around seven years old dressed ready for the school Christmas party. I was dressed in a brown and cream full length party dress. They were popular colours that year but I didn't like my dress or the colour. There would be no point in complaining as it was all I had. We were spoiled with gifts at Christmas. Three piles of presents on Christmas morning in the living room, we loved watching each other open the gifts and share the joy of the morning. One year my brother received an inflatable dinghy and one morning before our parents woke, we inflated it in our living room. The three of us jumped inside it to watch children's television in the mornings of the school holidays. In my mind it was a strange present as we rarely went to the local beach as a family in the summer other than our two week holiday but we thought it was fun anyway. My maternal grandparents came to ours for Christmas lunch alternate years. They were both very tall and powerful people. They were really tall compared to my tiny Nana. They were always dressed well. My Grandfather dressed in his suit, shirt and tie and my Gran dressed in her tweed skirts and blouses. They had a stoical attitude and as children we were expected to behave and remain quiet in their presence! One year, during our Christmas meal at home, my step-Gran fell off the three legged stool she was sitting on and fell on top of me after a few too many glasses of Sherry. As children we thought this was hilarious but Mam was hysterical as she briskly helped my step-Gran up. I was a little shocked but I wasn't hurt. There was never a dull moment in our house.

During school holidays my Mam and great Aunt would venture to town or the coast with me and have lunch out a few times a year and I loved it. Just me and them, my brothers must have been elsewhere or school. We would have our lunch at the same restaurant and our order would always be plaice and chips. The treats weren't easily afforded but we felt we had everything a young family needed in the '70's / 80's. Shopping trips and treats were rare and exciting. This made them be all the more appreciated when they did happen.

I felt I was never too big to talk to Dad or ask for a cuddle as he never declined my request. I was tall, lean and energetic, and he nicknamed me 'spaghetti long legs.' Once we had fidgeted to gain a comfortable spot on the armchair he used to sit with his arms loosely around me, watching television. Safe and quiet. I used to watch him smoke his cigarettes. Smoke puffing out and around us as he exhaled, slowly taking its time to move away from his face and eyes. His eyes squinted. A stupid thing I thought but I still tried smoking aged fifteen. Thankfully it wasn't for me. I put the remaining ones in my bag to sell them at school. I thought of the huge profit I would make for sure selling them individually. I never really liked Dad smoking and thankfully he stopped smoking on my brother's eighteenth birthday.

I must have been fourteen years old when I stopped sitting on his knee. I only stopped then because I was nearly as tall as him. My legs dangling awkwardly over his. I was fourteen years old when my older brother handed his Saturday evening paper round to me. The football paper. He was always out with friends now, aged eighteen. He liked to play pool and ended up with numerous trophies in his room. Two long shelves full. The paper round he had developed was an hour's work with fifteen to twenty pounds profit in tips. It was a well thought out route. I was always active. I would speed house to house on my roller boots or use the bike my younger brother had custom built from parts he'd also 'found'.

One Saturday, I overheard some boys from school calling me names and being unkind to me. I heard them being mean and derogatory about how sporty and tomboyish I was. As I was as I rode past them on my loyal and worthwhile mission I was able to ignore their comments although it made me think for a moment that I was a little different from my peers. There was a lot of money to be collected and twenty pounds was a lot of money then and it would end up in my pocket so that was my focus. I also provided childcare for neighbours children and some friends' children that my Dads knew from work most Saturdays so that was extra pocket money too.

I loved my brothers; they were good to me and they always protected me when we were outside or at school. My brother found the cigarettes though. I'd forgotten about them. I saw his anger as he crumpled the packet and with it I saw the profit crumble onto the floor. It was now dealt with though and there was no further punishment. Relief.

My youngest brother went away for a weekend to Blackpool. He was probably eighteen years old. He showed us his new tattoo proudly on his return. He has a lovely cheeky smile. I was really upset - A TATTOO?! My brother? It was the early 1980's and tattoos weren't so popular then. I didn't actually know anyone with a tattoo. Now, more than thirty years later they seem so popular that it's trickier to find anyone without one. I love looking at peoples' different choices and combinations of tattoos and the stories that go with them. Back then though I was quite sensitive, I just burst into tears. I just didn't like them at that time. I liked how he was. He had little biceps that he was currently developing using the weights and huge punch bag which hung from the garage rafters. He used to drink a mixture of raw eggs and milk to build his muscles. To me he was perfect. How could he harm his beautiful fair skin? My lovely brother.

Mam went crazy and went to the kitchen and returned with a scourer. He laughed so much. He had us all taken in with his tricks again! It was a fake tattoo! He was and still is the biggest joker. Our very own Peter Pan. We adore each other and our children are very close to each other also. He is reliable, conscientious, creative and cares alot about his family.

I was active at school, studious, average intelligence at least or that was my perception. Every exam I passed I had worked towards for a significant time. Unlike my brothers I did study a lot. My brother would tease me when I was studying but I actually enjoyed learning. I chose my career at twelve years old. A lovely school friend that I adored, worked with me on a career project. I researched careers and realised my path and my mind was set. I wanted to be a midwife. We studied hard but we played hard too. I ran with this friend from the age of fourteen years old. Most school mornings we would meet at 7am. We'd meet half way between our houses which were about two kilometres apart. There were no mobile phones then so we chose the same days and the same time which would allow us time to shower and change for school. We were always dedicated to our plans and committed to each other for a couple of years. Initially, we had no knowledge or training plan but then we decided to run a local half marathon. Why not? After all, we were soon to be sixteen. It was a good plan. We were determined and brave. We persevered through the winter, rain and wind and frosty mornings and into the warm and bright spring mornings.

    I didn't know at that age that all of those qualities that we were developing in us would be our strengths which would last into adulthood. They would stay with me in my heart and I'd call on them. They would actually end up saving me in the end. The health professionals I'd come in contact with during my illness would support me and keep me safe but my core values would save me. I would save myself.

CHAPTER TWO
RUN DEB RUN

I loved running from being very small. I Would run in the back street, race classmates in the playground, but my running as a youngster didn't lead me anywhere apart from coming first position once in a run across the moor during a triathlon aged fifteen years old. My school running partner moved away after we left school and my social life had taken precedence in my young adulthood. When I was older and my precious children were past the baby stage, I wanted some 'me' time again. I had devoted myself to my children and rarely went out when they were young. They followed me everywhere for years, even to the bathroom. Sometimes I did wish for a moment's peace or an uninterrupted bath. I just love being a Mam so I always had them with me unless I was working. So cute, so precious, polite and well behaved mostly! I felt so blessed to have three beautiful and wonderful daughters.

I was thirty two when a neighbour's sister in law died of breast cancer and I felt some of the pain and compassion for my friend and the family she left behind. She was very young. Helplessly I looked at the situation. I thought of doing something to help others in similar situations suffering from breast cancer. I told my friend that I would run the local half marathon with her for a breast cancer charity later in the year. Helping others is frequently my motivator in my life and I committed myself to it but I couldn't even run around our small estate at that time which takes around three minutes! My energy and enthusiasm were endless at this time and she agreed to join me in the half marathon, it was her first time, my second.

It took about nine months of training, gradually building up our time on our feet. Our running distance increased gradually and our bodies adjusted to the exertion. We didn't know our limits and how our bodies would cope with the half marathon. Some training sessions would be tough and painful. Painful breathing became a problem especially for my friend as she developed exercise induced asthma. She often wheezed during our whole route. I had to stop myself asking repeatedly if she was okay as her breathing was so noisy and trust in her to identify it becoming a serious issue. After a few doctors appointments and some regular medication the asthma was under control and she continued to train well. Overall our training went fairly well and the sponsorship I was accepted for was a good motivator. As the training progressed I struggled with painful legs as I developed agonising shin splints. It seemed that as a result of increasing the distances of our runs too quickly and from overpronation that I strained my legs. I had to stop running but I cycled and swam to keep my fitness up until my shin splints became manageable a few weeks later. I then took up my training again to prepare for the race in time. British weather can also be a challenge but come rain or shine we'd be out training. I don't ever back out of commitments. I ran for the charity 'Breakthrough Breast Cancer '. This part of the charity was involved in research into breast cancer and I felt it was important in order to improve the future for breast cancer sufferers. I wouldn't let these people down. And I wouldn't abandon my friend, we were in this together.

    The run day went fairly well. No major difficulties except for the last few kilometres which were uphill and my friend found this challenging. She was low on energy and struggling to continue running. I stayed with her. I wasn't going to leave her now. With some encouragement we completed the run. We were elated by our achievement and it was my second half marathon. Nearly twenty years after the first, I ran a very similar time. No slower twenty years on. This was a good result for me and six hundred pounds raised for the charity. Nice. There was an added bonus too as I entered the charity tent at the end of the race for refreshments. I was given a leg massage on a treatment couch and it felt so good after running for over two hours. We soon met up with our families and wore our new tee shirts and medals with immense pride. Once I got home, my hips were very sore but my legs felt great after the massage. It was a struggle to get up the stairs to bed but I managed and felt great delight of our achievement.

    We ran on and off after that for a short time before we went our separate ways. I don't recall why we did this as we ran at a good pace together.

We had different commitments with our children and our different work. As I said, 'I'm okay' in my own company. I ran for miles with music as my motivator. It's a flexible sport, fitting in around my work and my husband's shift work and the needs of my children.

The concentration involved in running outside led to me being de-stressed also. I found it would straighten out any worrying thoughts and level out stresses building up inside after a non-stop or challenging day at home or work. I encouraged my youngest brother to run and he ran for years and still goes to the gym regularly. It helps him stay strong mentally too.

As some work stresses started to build, I realised my mood was lowering and I was becoming tired so I needed a plan to motivate me. I hadn't experienced anything like this before, so I decided to take action and I applied for a small local ten kilometre race that I'd also run a few years before. There were only two thousand online entries accepted but every year that I'd applied I'd been allocated a place. This year was no exception. I was given a place to run the race. I had something to focus on and started to train. My mood was difficult. I was anxious but very low and I was considering taking sick leave from my role as a community midwife. I was becoming exhausted. I began to feel drained after running and wasn't feeling the feel good endorphins that I usually felt after a run and hot shower. I would usually run before work or run early in the mornings of my days off from work so I could shower and enjoy the rest of my day. But this wasn't happening, not now, I knew I was lucky to have a place in the race so I kept going with my training. I was quite determined and disciplined with any running schedule that I'd set my mind to. My knowledge of improving my diet and ways to improve my pace was limited but I accepted this and didn't put too much pressure on myself. I put just enough pressure to keep myself training. I just kept going. With perseverance I would usually reach whatever goal I set myself.

    A few half marathons and local ten kilometre runs were my limit though. I felt that I didn't want to train for more than these distances due to the demands and length of training required. I preferred training for half marathon distances. I felt this was enough to challenge my body and mind. I loved improving my distances in training and reaching the point where I felt like a machine; my breathing steady and my heart no longer pounding with the strain of the exertion.

    The years that I was training for the half marathon I would even take my running kit on our two week summer holiday. I would set my alarm at 6.30am whilst my husband and girls were sleeping. My favourite place to run abroad was Spain. I would make my way to the cycle path that encompassed the coastal road. As I ran, the sun would rise above an opposing mountain and I soaked in the beauty of the view and the warmth on my body. The breeze was always slight and the sky a beautiful bright blue, rarely a cloud in the sky. I felt really happy running in this picturesque environment. I was proud of my dedication to my training schedule and my devotion to running and knowing I was optimising my future health. Before heading back to our apartment, I would take my shoes and socks off and head into the sea. I would paddle up to thigh high water and it felt wonderful on my tired legs. It was so refreshing. I would sit on the shoreline afterwards and enjoy the moment as my legs quickly dried in the morning sunshine. As I ran back to our apartment I really savoured the time alone. On reaching the poolside, I would step under the cold shower and feel invigorated and ready for my day ahead with my wonderful family.

   This year though when I became ill, training was not going as well as I planned. I lacked motivation and energy to get out and train. I was really fatigued all of the time. I had also begun to suffer sleeping difficulties; unable to sleep through the night without experiencing bad dreams. I felt unhappy. This was a new experience to me. I took a ten day break from running. I thought that a rest and time to recover would help if my body was objecting to me burning the candle at both ends due to a busy family life and a community caseload to manage. I thought that maybe that was all that I needed. I worked long hours at work then did hours of paperwork after my working day. No time was allocated on the working day for paperwork despite me asking management for it. I went from house to house and then on to my antenatal clinics. Busy days. I thought that ten days seemed to be enough time to recalibrate and restart without missing too much time training which would then mean I could continue to train up in time for the race. I restarted with some enthusiasm but this soon wavered and I struggled to improve my distance. I felt flat after a training session. I became disheartened and confused. I do recall reading that moderate exercise can uplift mood and heal mild or moderate depression and is as good as or better than antidepressants. So I ate healthier and I ran again. I was unsure of what was happening to me. Then, time became blurred as my health deteriorated. My threshold for crying was definitely lowered. I recall crying at work and feeling sad a lot of the time. I would be eating a meal at home with my young children and I would suddenly end up in tears as we sat at the table and they would sit and stare not knowing what to say or do as they were still young. When my mood didn't improve over the next few weeks, I visited the doctor. I didn't realise until I sat in her chair how much pressure I'd been under. I blurted it all out. All the reasons I thought my mood to be low. I cried uncontrollably. I wasn't very coherent. I was probably her worst and most distressed patient that day. I left for home to wait for talking therapy or counselling, whichever was available first. She informed me it could be in about eight weeks. I started my first antidepressant which would work within six weeks. I still didn't understand how or why this had happened to me.

    I forced myself to put on my running kit. I reduced my training schedule and managed some short runs. It was hard. Not just hard like when your dry throat burns after cross country in P.E. at school. It was as if my mind had decided to run but then my body and mind weren't synchronised and my legs just wouldn't run. Sometimes my mood would plummet during a run and I would feel like curling up on the ground into a fetal position and weeping into my hands. I had visions of me collapsing on the street as a result of exhaustion as I became defeated in my efforts to run. I didn't know at the time but this was a result of me ruminating about the appalling situation I perceived myself to be in as I ran.

    A good friend from work with whom I'd run some races with previously, used to encourage me to run with her. She inspired me to keep going, to run as we always had. I had started to run with her through a very difficult period in her career as a midwife. It made her unwell for quite a few months. I'd collect her in my car and we'd run at the park. We'd talk as we ran and afterwards we travelled to her house where we drank a lot of coffee and talked for hours. She returned to work after her stressful episode and we continued to run for a long time together. Now I was struggling to stay in the running partnership. Occasionally our zest to get up and run would naturally dwindle but soon we found our desire again to meet and run and talk. We became very close friends. I think it was tough for her when I was ill. She had been ill and recovered and we knew of some of the difficulties such an illness brought. I can say anything to her and have never heard unhelpful statements said to me, unlike from others. Always truth and wisdom. She is very special to me. My friend sometimes didn't say much and that was ok. Sometimes, a hug would be more powerful than struggling to find the right words to help.

I recall a different work colleague who had also enjoyed running for a long time but had found herself not being able to run with the same ease once her beloved mum died. She was bereft and sobbed and broke down after her runs. She still continued but I recalled how she had described this difficulty one quiet day at work. She told me how she struggled. I remembered our conversation and it resonated with me. I kept running. If she could do it I could too. She inspired me to stay in control and help myself. This was a problem I hadn't ever had before. I was physically the perfect build to run. Long legs, tall, slim build. I liked running, I had a race to run.

When my running became difficult I tried stride counting. In desperation I tried to count each step as I ran them. It took four or five attempts to count to one hundred without forgetting which number I was up to as my concentration was so poor now. I began to realise I wasn't well. I was frightened to stop running. It was the only self-help method I knew in the early stages of my deteriorating health. Hundreds of strides I counted, hundreds and then hundreds more, pure desperation to keep going. At this point I had hope; I hoped the exercise would help me.

Throughout my running years I had rarely stopped in a training session. I had pride. I was more likely to bend down and tie my shoe lace that didn't need tying instead of ever walking in my running kit. People were mean if you stopped. Car and van horns would sound to let me know they saw me walking and I would feel self-conscious as a result. Even through one of the half marathons I felt faint and dizzy around the sixteen kilometre mark. My legs felt like jelly and I felt as though I'd fall to the ground. I didn't walk. I ate glucose tablets that became powder in my dry gasping mouth. I wouldn't walk. I staggered on until the glucose worked and the feeling passed. Then I gathered pace and held my head up high as I ran through the finish line. It was a great achievement of my intended goal.

I just kept on counting steps and hoping that I'd soon be home. It was a particularly rainy year. I often came home soaked to the skin. Soon though, I started to fall asleep after running. There were no positive endorphins detected, just pure exhaustion. In retrospect, I think I had burnout at this point. Despite this, I did eventually reach my goal that year in training. Ten kilometres I built up to. I'd never win but I'd make the race that year without stopping. By counting, running, persevering. Two weeks before race day nature stepped in. I started with a cold and it worsened and took hold of my chest, it was so sore. I was affected by a viral infection. This worsened my asthma and made it unmanageable without my medication. It was obvious to me that it wasn't wise to run the race. Devastated that my efforts were wasted and too late to change my place in the run to the following year. I was definitely out of the race.

    I was so disappointed; my huge and determined efforts that spanned months would be to no avail. It was the only thing that had kept me going and I wouldn't even get my new run tee shirt! My health plummeted to awful depths. I was definitely out of the race. I withdrew. Heart broken. My mind was broken too and I knew it.

CHAPTER THREE
MY WORK

I honestly felt that my career was a calling. I remember the very moment I decided, as a teenager, on my chosen vocation. I studied hard at school and passed all of my 'O levels' and 'GSCEs' and then went to the local college on a local pre-nursing course. This course enabled me to study 'A levels' and have a day release at the local hospital for the very first time. This was so much fun aged seventeen years old and at eighteen years I became a student nurse.

    The first year of college was spent attending a lot of nights out socialising with my new college friends and not nearly enough studying. I just passed my first year exams and it was a shock that my marks were only just acceptable for the first time in my life. As a result I effectively studied for a two year course in one year and that resulted in me feeling a lot of pressure. I did pass my 'A Levels' a year later and it was a great relief.

    It was the Christmas before I started my nursing training that I met my husband. He was about to start working as a trainee Police Officer in London and I had my nursing place for later that year. We commuted for five years between our home town and London and had a great social life. We had so much fun staying at our friends flat or at the Police Section house. I sneaked into his room after secretly passing the concierge. We were so happy together and we were engaged six months after meeting each other much to my parents' concern as I was only eighteen and he was seven years my senior. But I knew we were good for each other. I felt that when I met him he was who I'd been waiting for. I knew that we would end up together. Our relationship quickly flourished and we felt we had known each other for years, even after a few months. After six months we were engaged.

During my student nurse training I found that most of the nursing ward Sisters at that time were very stoical and matriarchal. We treat them with a lot of respect. One particular ward Sister took her students under her wing and taught us all so much and empowered us to work confidently. She was a beautiful person and a great role model. I recall her fondly; she was energetic, inspiring and encouraging towards all of her students. We had great fun and I still have a photo of a few of us working on the medical ward on Christmas Day with my student nurse friends and her. It was our first Christmas of many that we would work in our NHS careers. We wore our starched, white hats and white dresses with pride. My good friend who was a student nurse used to starch our hats in batches as she did them perfectly. Our efforts were hilarious as they drooped to one side or the other. Our hats would often become tangled in our patients' privacy curtains as we cared for their needs. We had so much fun and were welcomed in our new roles. There were four of us that became very close friends.

We studied hard for three years as we rotated to different areas in the hospital gaining our experience and each year gaining an extra bright orange stripe for our white hats. I loved surgical and post operative care the best. Wound dressings and inserting naso-gastric tubes were my favourite chores. Seeing the wounds improve with the benefits of the most up to date dressings was very satisfying.

I loved this time of my life but I am now embarrassed at how young and naive I was on qualifying as a registered general nurse at age twenty one. I'd led a sheltered straightforward life until that point. I had a lot still to learn about people and their lives and illnesses and there was definitely personal development to achieve. I knew I wouldn't be nursing long because it wasn't my long term dream. I just knew that I was going to be a midwife.

When I secured my contract as a newly qualified nurse we bought our first house thirty miles away from our hometown where my husband was transferred to work. I travelled for a year doing nursing at the hospital staying at our new home then I was successfully given a place to do my midwifery training near our new home and we were married.

I was well supported during my midwifery training and I thrived. I met some great practitioners; midwives and doctors alike were supportive and it created great learning environments. I initially watched ten normal births and then conducted deliveries myself with my mentor at hand if any difficulties arose. I was in total awe of the strength and courage that women showed in their labours. Their innate, mammalian impulses and sheer determination resulted in them birthing their new-born's into the world. I was astounded at the way their pain disappeared immediately once the baby was born and how pain was replaced with joy on placing their newborn into their arms. I was in my element seeing how beautiful their baby's were. The whole process simply amazed me. The precious moment they held their child for the time melted my heart and in the early days a tear would appear in my eyes as I was filled with the pureness and the beauty of the birth experience and indeed the miracle that birth is. As I conducted the necessary forty births myself in my training I was then ready to deliver babies alone and provide all the necessary emotional support which empowers the women I care for. Soon, the tears of happiness no longer came to me; it developed into pride and humbleness I felt as a result of being a part of the lives of the families I cared for. This never left me, and I felt great respect for the women I cared for. My career was a big part of who I was. I adored the mothers and their babies. I loved watching the first breaths as the baby adjusted to the outside world. I developed an interest in supporting mothers with their feeding methods and particularly supporting new mothers to breastfeed correctly. I continued to support the mothers post operatively after caesarean of instrumental deliveries with tenderness, patience and positivity.

   Obviously, there were sad times too but the pain of these situations usually subsided over some time. I had dealt with lost pregnancies and late miscarriages on a number of occasions when I'd previously been based in the hospital. In my experiences of dealing with families who had experienced pregnancy losses, I worked with the situation for a day or two at the most. Then, the fast paced nature of the service we provided in the hospital would move us on to the next family to be cared for. There was a lot of expectation to cope and continue.

CHAPTER FOUR
THE NEWSFLASH

   I tried to reason with myself and make logic of the sadness that I'd started to feel. My old Grandad had died the previous year. I must be grieving still for him or not dealing with the grieving process fully at the time I thought as I was abroad when he died and also when it was his funeral. I wanted to travel home to say goodbye but in my heart I knew I could say goodbye spiritually wherever I was. We loved talking about our holiday plans. He knew we were going to our favourite holiday destination and he loved his holidays too so I thought it was best that we carried on with our plans. So I stayed abroad and spent the time of his funeral floating alone in the sea thinking of all our shared and happy times. I recalled the many times I would call by his house that he shared with his second wife. I would telephone ahead to check they were home and I would call by for my thirty minute meal break at work and always an overdue visit to their toilet. My step Gran would hold her stomach when I appeared at the door and always joke about needing the midwife and how lovely it was to see me. We chatted for hours on my days off too, I was very close to them.
   I think he would have liked me enjoying my holiday instead of being sad at his funeral. He was our patriarch and I loved him a lot. I was grieving; that's why I was sad. I was aware it was six weeks since my mood was low and flat. I was tearful at

home too. It must be a delayed reaction. I tried to find logic in my level of sadness. Grief for my other Grandparents had settled to manageable levels around six weeks after their passing. Grandad was an amazing man. He was blind with old age but his mind was still clear. He knew which petrol station to get the cheapest petrol and which bus to get to any destination. He knew which road to travel to any location in the U.K. He was in his nineties and travelled around the country on coach trips. His last venture was meant to be only days before his sudden death. The only things that confused him were the price of his travel insurance and 'Why shouldn't you iron jumpers?' He was on high blood pressure medication so of course he didn't have blood pressure problems so why was his insurance so pricey? He was a bold and cheeky character and we missed him a lot, but I knew that the major catalyst which played a huge part in the emotional burden that I started to carry as a result of work was an unexpected and unexplained murder of a baby.

I had been working with the family for many months prior to this devastating event. There had been no warning signs that put me in a position to prevent this tragedy. I learned of the murder on the local news. I wasn't at work that day. It was the last day of my annual leave. I stood in shock staring at the television and I immediately recognised the house on the news report.

The footage of the street and the house where the murder had taken place was shown. I

immediately recognised the street. 'OH NO!' I gasped out loud. WHAT has happened? My mind raced but I didn't initially know which family it involved. There were no issues in this street...
Who the hell?
What the hell?
    My jaw dropped. I was aghast. Horrified at what I saw and heard. I rushed into my home study and retrieved my work diary. The age of the baby was given in the news report. I rapidly thumbed the pages. It took me a few minutes to look through the lists of families and addresses that I attended day in, day out. I spotted the mothers name, there it was in my handwriting; the address which reminded me of the visit to the house.
'NO!' I exclaimed.
    My book fell from my hands, my knees buckled and gave way and I was on my knees. Head bowed forward, hands on the floor as my only support. I felt total disbelief and was in total shock. I remembered that I had stopped working with the family only a few weeks before. I recalled my last visit with them. The details of the living room, the new baby items neatly piled around the room, me undressing and weighing the baby and redressing the baby and cherishing a little hug as I handed the baby back to the mother. I recalled the baby's name. I recalled the family support she had and who was present.
I sobbed and sobbed.
How could this have happened?

That week, back at work, I had to make a statement at the request of the police. All of my paperwork connected to the family was taken from me as evidence. To this day, many years later, I recall the family, the baby's name and what their house was like.

Months after the murder, I sympathised with the grieving family members as I cared for another pregnant family member. I couldn't ask questions of the incident as it would be a case to be heard in crown court. I felt that I couldn't do the visit without a cascade of emotions flooding me as I left their property. Tears rolled down my cheeks as I drove away heading for my next house call; leaving them in their grief and myself suffering vicarious grief.
I spoke to one of my managers about my upset at dealing with this family again but she said I'd been asked by the family to care for the pregnant relative. So I continued.

A sudden death or murder is very difficult to comprehend in my mind and this was absolutely dreadful; this was a baby murder. We didn't know who had murdered the baby and wouldn't know for a long time until a verdict was made in court. It was the worst thing I've ever dealt with in all of my life. A severe and untoward incident which would take such a long time to be investigated and had a life changing effect on me.

I saw my co-workers at the surgery afterwards and could see they were affected too. They were devastated and it had a negative impact on their working lives. Individually, they dealt with it in different ways. Most of them took time away from work on sick leave to some degree after the murder. As health professionals involved in the case, we dealt with our feelings of trauma and despair in isolation as we were all told we were going to be witnesses at the trial. We were not allowed to discuss the murder with each other. As the after effects unfolded, it made me think that health professionals who have had input and work alongside families prior to an event like this are definitely a forgotten group. As the details of the crime unfolded, I was in disbelief that there was no specific or specialist support available for those affected by crime, especially of this severity. The culture of the NHS was deeply embedded in me by this time. To disregard my feelings and continue in a professional manner was my way of life at work, regardless of the circumstances. So I thought I should continue at work as was always expected after such experiences. I worked on for a year until I had a mental health crisis. It was very deeply felt, like nothing I'd ever experienced. I believed this to be because the professional relationship had developed with the family over the full pregnancy and onto the meeting of the newborn before the baby died. I have always felt things very deeply and had deep compassion since being a little child and I believe some people do feel things more deeply than others.

    Over time, information of the injuries that occurred to the baby prior to the death were disclosed to me by two managers and my mind stored this and I began clearly visualising the harm and subsequent death. My brain could take no more upset or strain. I developed intrusive thoughts and could visualise the injuries happening throughout my days for many months. I became an insomniac and had nightmares with themes of death, deaths of my children and of many tragedies in which I stood by helplessly.

CHAPTER FIVE
THE AFTERMATH

Initially, I contacted my union representative to find specialist counselling but to no avail. I asked my union and MIND's blue light support but to no avail. We considered private therapy but felt it was going to need comprehensive support to help me. So I decided to work with NHS mental health services. This was fragmented with long waiting times unfortunately.

In the wait for counselling from the occupational health department, I was told that I would be given six sessions and we did wonder though how I could continue every day with the acute distress and devastation I felt. It still affects me and comes into my life in various forms twelve years on. A news report of a child murder, a comment from a parent to a child in a derogatory manner, a distressed or hysterically crying child, or a parent annoyed with a child, a sad looking child or a child with the same name as the child who was murdered. They all take my thoughts for a while, hijacking my mind, distracting me and testing my tolerance and mental stability.

When I left work knowing I was unwell I did not for one second have knowledge of how long this episode would take. In retrospect this was a blessing as I don't think I would have endured this period of time knowing the struggles that were ahead of me. In my desperation to get appropriate help I said I'd see the local counsellor at the G.P surgery. It was only a four week wait, but as I unravelled my incoherent thoughts to her she nodded repeatedly. She was silent except to insist she could help. My intuition told me she couldn't; she really wanted to and seemed very kind but I knew my problems were way deeper than she could handle. I didn't tell her everything. I felt that she wouldn't cope with what I had to tell. I never went to see her again. But that left me without a plan for support in place. I felt lost.

I had empty days ahead of me. I left work and handed over my diary to my team leader to deal with. One day, soon after, I was so agitated and exhausted that I rang an old friend from work and when she heard my distress she came straight over. She helped me by ringing my G.P. surgery and organising an urgent appointment for me. I didn't even have the clarity to speak to the receptionist myself. It was the second of many doctor appointments and to this day I don't remember the outcome of that particular visit. It was a blur.

I was referred to the occupational health department by my manager when it was known that I was going to be absent from work for more than a few weeks. I was seen after a number of weeks by the nurse at the hospital. She listened and was kind and compassionate. I cried so much that I used all of her tissues.

My body was so tired I could hardly sit up. My head was heavy with a denseness of the depressive mood. My stomach felt tense and painful. I found it hard to describe how it felt; it felt much worse than a bad mood, very different from anything I'd experienced before. I had an awful feeling that I perceived impending doom to be like. I apologised for my state and my lack of control over myself. I remember feeling ashamed that I failed to cope with my emotions as I'd always been expected to do as a nurse and midwife. I don't recall what was said. I didn't have a plan at this stage. My situation was just like a confused and jumbled mess. I had no idea what my future had in store for me and I don't think they knew either. The occupational health nurses were very good support. Sadly, I slipped through their review net and I wasn't seen by them for another five months. At the nurse appointment I had begged for counselling. I was put on a five to six week waiting list but I think I was seen by her around four weeks after she'd taken a history over the phone. She was a helpful checking in point and it gave me some sort of structure for my one hour weekly appointment. She helped me analyse my low mood each visit and assess if I was in danger of harming myself. She tried to assist me to organise my thoughts and my understanding of why I was so depressed. Round and round my thoughts went relentlessly. My thoughts were chaotic and were making no sense to me. My thought processes were absolute pandemonium.

Needless to say that the work counselling didn't help improve my low mood at all but it was a place to express my feelings out loud and to try and make sense of it. I had no clue what else to do and it just didn't help me. I couldn't think straight and felt in shock at everything that had happened and to suddenly be so ill. I felt very very sad. I was usually so enthusiastic, fun and lively with a contagious zest for life.

The counselling available through my work came quite quickly but I felt desperate to do something to help myself and not be trapped in this dire state of mind. I looked for books about depression with personal stories/memoirs about people suffering depression so I could compare what other people had felt and how they coped. Reading during the depression was so difficult. My concentration was poor and my cognition was definitely affected too. It was impossible to remember what I'd read and make any sense of it. Periodically I would try again but it would be a long time before these symptoms improved. I started journaling to unravel some thoughts, which developed into this book.

Before medication was found to suit and stabilise me, there was an occasion I felt desperate to find the specialist help that I needed. I was agitated, anxious, severely depressed and very distressed. The chaotic thoughts reigned again. I rang the local mental health crisis team and once again I had been reduced to tears as I tried to explain myself. I knew that I needed professional help but nothing was really improving with counselling or at the G.P surgery. As I was unable to speak on the phone, they asked to see me in person. I felt as if I would get appropriate help and support there. I drove a short distance to be assessed and I was hopeful that a plan to help me would be made. I'm usually a cooperative person but after a long and distressing conversation the practitioner assessed my mood as severely depressed and that I had no intention of harming myself or anyone else at that point. She asked if I was happy with a plan to go home and wait for standard talking therapy which had a long waiting list of nine months. 'Was I happy?' I was in disbelief and I really wasn't okay with the plan but it was the only option given to me. I knew I needed specialist help but I didn't know how I'd survive the wait. I didn't know where to find the right help. I drove home with tears streaming down my face. I had lost hope of ever getting fixed and wished for the first time that I was dead rather than feel this acute distress daily.

During my illness I was told by some people such words as 'You are worrying too much,' 'you need to be tougher,' 'what's in the past is the past.' I found this really insulting and quite offensive and it often angered me that they thought it was their right to analyse me. No one initially knew how ill I was feeling inside. I was so very ill and couldn't make sense of it myself for a long time so I realised it was impossible how others could have understood my frame of mind.

They had no clue.

CHAPTER SIX
MY ILLNESS

There were so many unpleasant symptoms. At first I slept a lot in the day; probably exhaustion or burnout I now believe. My mood was dire. I felt so ill and I was desperate to get 'something' fixed but didn't know exactly what was broken. I tried to comprehend that I had an illness. In my depression there was a mix of trauma and work stresses that were incomprehensible to a lot of the people that knew me, even my husband. It wasn't one incident or change in circumstances that made me ill but the accumulation of numerous things and a definite lack of support by my managers at the time. To meet friends or go to the shops became a challenge. Meeting friends meant addressing my feelings once again as they enquired how I was. I ignored a lot of thoughts and feelings. It was obvious colleagues and friends would ask regarding my health and wellbeing. I know they cared. Each and every one that contacted me or invited me for coffee or a walk; they cared. They may be shocked at seeing someone thin. I couldn't tolerate food. I was so pale with significant black circles under their eyes and a sad facial expression. I felt nothing but sadness and emptiness. I still only occasionally bothered to wash my hair. I had deserted my make-up. Too much energy to think about applying it and for no benefit. I would still look and feel awful even if I had bothered with my appearance.

When I had to go shopping, I didn't look at anyone. I became agitated and overstimulated standing in queues. In this stillness I'd often notice babies and toddlers. A lot were upset. Probably only bored or hungry my good friend pointed out when she accompanied me. My broken mind didn't like or process their distress well. My switch flicked to the distress of the murdered child prior to its death. Whimpering, crying, screaming. I needed to go home. Exhausted once again. Efforts wasted; more distress. My thoughts were awful and dark but at home I was not assessed or observed. I felt safe.

Bedtime was often a hopeful time. Although now I'm not sure why. I quite looked forward to it. Firstly, I thought a new day could possibly bring improvement and maybe one night my brain would actually switch to standby. Frustratingly, peace rarely came to me at night.

Nightmares occurred most nights. Nightmares of death, murder, car accidents, random dead people found around my property. As well as people hurting my children were the nightmares I suffered. The associated complex thoughts and feelings exhausted me and caused upset and turmoil. There was no freedom from being ill. My life had turned into chaos. It was relentless. I often woke up screaming, shouting or just confused. Strangely, I rarely cried as a result of the nightmares. It did disturb me though. I often stayed awake for hours after a nightmare. Some nights were quite unmanageable. My husband was exhausted and slept very well. I wished he would sit with me in the dark nights. I was scared for my own safety during the nights. I believed insomnia with a deep suicidal depression would make me lose comprehension and act hastily as the pain and tiredness escalate to unmanageable levels.

After some eleven or twelve months of suffering some of the pain left which was a small improvement; I no longer feared the night. I just lay awake for hours just waiting for a few hours of sleep or the sunrise to come. Sunrise was definite in all of this. I'd start another unpredictable and exhausting day. I would survive the night. The thoughts, they weren't real. I had 'insight' I was told professionally. I assume this was reassuring to health workers who became entangled in my situation as they tried to help me. I did fear losing insight; I visualised my death often. My death; a result of some hasty plan and impulsive action. A moment of confusion, doom or extreme hopelessness. It felt like a real risk that I would one day lose my tolerance and slight hope of ever improving and this was still my fear. It wasn't my life anymore.

As the months passed by, my brain was continually malfunctioning. I didn't want to be analysed but in being assessed I prayed someone would clarify what was going on. I actually could feel my heart was now totally broken. But I had to try and remember that my heart and character had also resulted in me being a good, kind, compassionate and honest person in the past. So I wouldn't be changing my 'sensitive heart.' I was me and I always would be. I had been proud of who I was. I wasn't now but I had been. I had been changed by this illness. I may have been shaped, altered and scarred but I was inside there and I looked from inside myself out to the world.

   I managed the depression by breaking each day into segments of time. Depending on the severity of the feelings and potential doom, I would manage my life half hour by half hour on a difficult day; hour by hour on a bad day. After months of learning how it affected me I realised it was still quite unpredictable day by day. Sometimes I felt suffocated by impending doom. I was edgy and agitated by these feelings and thoughts which infused into my mind through no request I'd ever made.

   I usually managed or coped with stressful situations that happen randomly in life quite well. Although, I did have a slight anxious trait from being a teenager which started with pressure from myself creating exam stress as I wanted to gain good results which would be my gateway to my envisaged career. Once depression set in, I would manage at the time of stress but then my mood would drop to very uncomfortable levels and I'd once again feel drained and distressed or cry. My threshold for crying was definitely lowered during the illness.

   The changes in my mood throughout some days were too numerous to comprehend. My dismal mood could have lasted for the whole day, whole week or some hours through one day. This lack of control and unpredictability was one of the hardest aspects of it. Not knowing when the feelings would even improve or if they would ever go away. One lunchtime I was making myself a sandwich and had gathered everything that I needed but when it came to making it I became confused and my husband stood watching from the other side of the kitchen. I became frustrated and angry that he wouldn't help me. So I took aim with my mayonnaise and squirted him in the chest. He was shocked at my actions as it was so unlike me. Then we both looked at his tee shirt and the mayonnaise was all over the right side of his chest. Right in the heart. It made me laugh but he was very upset that I had dirtied his good tee-shirt with oily mayonnaise. He quickly forgave me and sat me down and made my sandwich for me.

After over one year of persistent symptoms of depression, unrelieved by the many different medications, it becomes a part of you. Clinging onto you without an invite. I learned to carry on with day to day activities. Often hiding my true feelings as it was easier than dealing with them. I suffered continuously especially in the first years of the illness as I tried around seven antidepressants without any relief of the depressive symptoms. Some of the medication gave me side effects but I would pray and hope that one of them would help and I would heal and the illness would go away. But in truth I didn't know whether I was fixable.

A manager came to my home for the first time after I'd been absent from work for six weeks but the next time I saw her was after being off six months when she brought a human resource worker to discuss with me that my pay was halving. The support I received was poor. I had never been off work so long in my whole career. I was rarely sick except for a couple of chest infections and a back injury as a young student nurse. The lack of contact from management at my work at that time was a cause of great distress. I had worked there for around sixteen years. I tried to understand this as well as a lot of other issues around the illness. Did they have to be careful not to be seen as hassling sick employees? Or be careful not to make me feel worse? Or was there no care about my welfare from my managers that I'd been loyal to all of these years? I could make no sense of it. I felt extremely upset that it seemed that I was out of sight and out of their minds. I felt unsupported at the worst time of my life. It took a lot of courage on my behalf to telephone my manager. I tried a couple of times to ring but with no answer phone my calls were left unanswered. So I updated her by text with information of my sick note dates and medication that I was trying. That was all I could manage.

 I thought of all of the extra hours I'd worked after my regular hours to make sure my clients in my caseload had everything that they needed. All of the lunch breaks that I'd skipped to do a couple of tasks that needed doing. The extra travelling time that I'd endured just because it had been decided to move our office base miles further away from our working area. The reason was so we could 'gel' with our other co-workers and reduce the number of team leaders. There wasn't even time to do anything with our colleagues or have a full conversation before we had to leave to return back to our geographical area once our daily visits were organised. To do your job well and be put under extra strain for reasons that don't seem valid is difficult everyday. But I had told the new team leader before I left I'd do the best I possibly could in the circumstances. I had worked under a lot of strain for around one year before I became unwell.

CHAPTER SEVEN
THE PATH OF DESTRUCTION

As I've started to heal, the pathway of the illness has become a little vague in my mind. I'm so thankful for this as it dulls the pain but it also means I don't clearly know when improvement or any healing actually happened. Some of my story continues to be entangled with confusion. I have an element of disbelief and difficulty finding acceptance that it happened to me. I had such a zest for life and exercise and running and my work and family before I was hit by depression. It was sudden; so sudden and painful that I clearly knew the cause but I was very confused as to how my mind had become so ill so quickly. Of course I'd been under some pressure at work but to cause this extent of damage? I was totally dumbfounded. I behaved normally at work, carrying out home visits, making decisions every day, managing a job that I'd practised for twenty five years. None of my colleagues had questioned anything.

One senior manager called me into her office when she saw me in the hospital corridor before I was ill but I was affected by what had happened and it was obviously showing on my face. She explained that I'd lost my smiling, shining eyes and asked what was happening. We had a conversation and I was allowed to leave with no follow up or offer of support. In retrospect I wish I'd written down my concerns in an email and pushed for further meetings, but as I was so busy I just continued as was expected by the culture of the NHS. In my work I worked with trainees. As I drove from call to call we chatted. We worked thoroughly with our clients. We were welcomed into their homes and often laughed with the clients in delight at the beauty and cleverness of the precious little babies we worked with. The enthusiasm I had was having a positive effect on the trainee's and their learning. The proud parents would willingly show us how their little ones were thriving. The new mothers would practise skin to skin and allow the baby unaided, to crawl up the mothers abdomen and kick in a determined effort to reach the breast to suckle. This birth crawl is easily seen immediately in a newborn given the time, especially once the sedative effect of the opiates given to the women in labour have worn off. The trainees' faces just lit up at the sight of the strength, and the babies showed their individuality and smiles for the first time. We felt that it was amazing to witness the beauty of it all and we were very lucky to be a part of it; it was an honourable position to be in. We were humbled to be a huge part of the families in the local vicinity. Life's little miracles we worked with. A product of only two little cells developing uniquely in every little person. It still astounds me every day when I see little babies, children or my growing children. In our community we would see many family members and over the ten years in this role I met a lot of amazing, clever, funny, kind, inspirational and also challenging people.

One day I had a house visit above some shops. It was a new call and I didn't know this family. When I arrived, it transpired that the pregnant lady had been in hospital with complications and I was to carry out the antenatal examination. I looked around on entering. It was the kind of place where it was better to wipe your feet on leaving than entering ! Sparsely furnished, debri spread across the sofa and floor. On the floor was a baby, around eighteen months old. I said hello to the baby and started chatting to him in a friendly high pitched voice as most people do to babies. He was laid on his back, feet resting on the sofa, dressed only in a nappy and a grubby unfastened vest. He was feeding himself his bottle of milk. He looked at me as I chatted away. Then he took the bottle out of his mouth and told me to 'fuck off!' My job wasn't always this shocking. Most of my days were very enjoyable. I dealt with many issues. An antenatal lady rang me because she had eaten an out of date yoghurt and was worried about it affecting the unborn. A postnatal lady rang me as she thought her nipple had fallen off using a breastpump, needless to say I rushed to see her to assess her and reassure her it hadn't but with some breastfeeding support she went on to successfully breastfeed her newborn. I related the benefits of breastfeeding to another pregnant lady. A reduction of infections is one benefit of breastfeeding in the newborn and one pregnant lady listened intently while we discussed the reality of breastfeeding. Her first baby had ended up in intensive care with pneumonia at only a few months old. She had bottle fed her first baby but wanted to breastfeed her second child to reduce the chances of this happening again as it had had a massive effect on the mothers mental health. She had a successful breastfeeding journey and was delighted with herself and it was so good to be a part of this. At one postnatal visit, new parents showed me their newborn and I was completing the newborn examination on the baby change mat and it promptly vomited a milky mucousy vomit and appeared to struggle to breath. I immediately and confidently lifted the baby and turned it face down to clear the birth mucous and patted its back until it recovered. The parents were very frightened and grateful that I'd been in attendance to assist at that time. Before I was ill I believe that I worked well and listened to what my clients needed. I liked being my own boss; tailoring my visits to who and where and when it was needed. I enjoyed the autonomy and empowering the families to do the best they could for their little ones. I educated families about the benefits of breastfeeding and stopping smoking. I started a breastfeeding support group in the community and taught feeding workshops. I was conscientious and worked hard. As most of my colleagues did.

    There was a lot of paperwork and appointment arranging involved in my work.I would ring the newly pregnant once they were home in the evening. I'd often work late into the night with piles of papers spread out on the carpet at home completing forms and forwarding letters. It wasn't unusual to do this; it's a complex job and there is no table big enough or time long enough for the job ever to be 'finished' during working hours. Initially, I didn't fret working into the evening. It would settle my girls into bed and work at a leisurely pace in the comfort of my home, peace of mind that it would all be in order once I'd finished. It was unpaid work after our contracted hours though which was not acknowledged by management at the time. Although we had known that actually at some point my colleagues would also be doing the same. Often seats and tables were taken up in the morning in the office by my colleagues. Nowhere to sit in my brief visit to the office. And my request to incorporate office time into my working week was declined by management.

After all, financial and time pressures were hitting all companies; the NHS was no different. Austerity was known to all workers whatever their role. On the ground level, time to complete client visits became limited as my individual client caseload rocketed. This was unpredictable and couldn't be controlled; it was just how it happened that year. I was knowingly working at least one third over my allocated capacity. I worked four days per week as I didn't want to commit to full time work with having three young children. In reality, if I'd calculated my hours worked it would have been well over my thirty hours per week.

I had an accurate record of the names of each client and when their babies were due. My caseload was one hundred and seventy clients that year and on the four day contract I should have had a caseload of much smaller numbers. To my disbelief my manager did her own calculation and disputed my numbers but I knew I was correct in my calculation.

Support from colleagues was intermittent depending on their commitments but also depending on their willingness too. Our work was difficult to plan exactly as new work was also added to our pre planned work on a daily basis. My determination was strong, my standards of work and conscientiousness didn't waiver. The logistics were often a challenge but this was a tricky year I was having. Or so I thought.

I'm not perfect but I had a passion for my job and I did my best as I worked alone in the community. I was intrigued by a lot of the families but I adored a lot more.

Suddenly the desire to continue and my ability to continue making good decisions came into question in my own mind as I wasn't feeling good emotionally. I became hypervigilant ensuring I made no errors in any way which would have added to my difficulties.

Then a lot of days became hard as pressures from an imperfect system built up against me. As a lone worker, apart from the company of trainee's sometimes, I expressed my concerns to management about the increased workload and the amount of safeguarding that I was involved with due to working in a low socioeconomic area.

Safeguarding was time consuming due to multidisciplinary meetings and increased paperwork and assessments. It either fell on deaf ears or maybe they thought the busy and difficult phase would just pass by. To this day, the people who should have helped me prior to the illness embedding itself within me have actually apologised since they saw how ill I became. I question whether they meant it. It didn't help me as it came too late.

I was feeling very vulnerable and fragile. I felt honoured to have the job I had but sadly it came into question whether I'd ever manage to do it again. I felt it was a lot to cope with all the physical and emotional demands that come with such a job working with families in their homes.

The long hard days didn't bring restful sleep as you may expect. I knew in my mind I needed a break, I was becoming very tired. I found myself planning my last week's work. I was on the edge. I had to be vigilant. I had to leave and go home and look after myself for a while.

CHAPTER EIGHT
HELP ME!

The illness was a living nightmare. Initially, I felt a feeling of doom and intrusive negative thoughts by day, the trauma of nightmares most nights. Nightmares are one of the most persistent symptoms I had for over thirteen years. It's not exactly the best start to any day with such thoughts of trauma or fear or helplessness diving around in your head as soon as you realise that you are awake. As well as sleeplessness, I felt despondent and exhausted when I woke at night after a disturbing sleep of two or three hours, knowing I'd be awake often till morning came.

Thankfully there were quite a few people who supported me through this illness. I am very grateful to my husband of over thirty years. At times I was filled with rage and argumentative with him as a result of secondary post traumatic stress disorder symptoms. That is, I was severely affected by trauma symptoms after hearing of the murder of a baby I had known but I wasn't directly involved. Other times I was guilt ridden that I was putting such strain on our marriage and I made myself believe he would leave soon because life with me was so difficult. He explained to me one day that I was a mere shell and he didn't know where his wife had gone with the big smile and laughing, shiny eyes. It broke my heart that I had destroyed our relationship and I had no strength to fix it. I'm so grateful to him for walking by my side through this illness and holding my hand in the dark times and keeping me safe from harm. Some days he had to take days off work to ensure my safety when I really struggled with my dire mood.

   He didn't give up. I'm very grateful that he kept our home clean and fed us when I really couldn't manage things. At other times I believed the illness was worsened by his desperate contributions to help or my mood would worsen after an argument. There were many arguments; he was frustrated and so was I. But he didn't give up on me when I was detached and ill. He didn't always understand me and he still didn't walk away from me when I had nothing inside me to give to him. My three beautiful daughters taught me a multitude of lessons and they hugged me and let me lie with them during the dark and agitating nights and never once complained. There were times they looked into my eyes as they cuddled me; they saved me many times. They also prompted me when my home keeping skills slipped and our home was a mess and I hadn't noticed while my husband was working. Their kind words and telling me they loved me and that I was a good Mam always helped me. I often thought I was unlovable and I felt guilty that I'd failed them. I love them all and will forever.

   My G.P. patiently listened and didn't judge me. She worked with me through this period and tried me with multiple antidepressants, sedatives and antihistamines (to make me drowsy) to find something to make my life safe whilst we dealt with the complexities of the situation. The simple act of writing appointments down and giving them to me in my hand was priceless through the daily distress and confusion. It ensured she kept in touch for assessments with me and didn't let me slip away from her busy clinics. I lacked motivation and suffered lethargy and an inability to organise my own appointments. She was compassionate and kind and caring throughout. Her honesty and empathy gave me direction and transparency that allowed us to make short term plans together. These plans were to be my stepping stones to recovery.

I have met a number of rushed, impatient and sarcastic G.P's in my personal and working life; I'm so grateful to my G.P. who wasn't one of them. She always believed I would heal and become well and have a stable mind once again and that I'd even enjoy life once again. She believed in me when I didn't believe in myself. I may have not made the journey to the other side without her. I feel forever in her debt.

She left the practice to work elsewhere when I was returning to work after eleven months of sick leave and she was delighted that I was starting to improve. Little did I know the improved episode wouldn't last. I saw another suitable and helpful, experienced G.P who was equally good to me and so I really appreciated this service. They were the only constant professional support I received, especially for the first eighteen months of the illness. Other mental health practitioners worked their allocated sessions with me and then moved on. I was never ashamed to ask for help when I was struggling which in retrospect was a strength and reassured practitioners that I was able to keep myself safe. But I was never sure of that for years.

Friends I'd had for years stood by me, some didn't. Some work colleagues that I didn't even know noticed me or cared about me contacted me. A couple of new friends that appeared in my life were really brilliant. I often wondered how they wanted to befriend an ill person who was always tired or yawning as they spoke. Maybe they could see 'me' inside even though I couldn't identify myself at that time. I felt like my personality and identity had been stolen because I was barely functioning and unable to work at this time. The guilt of me creating upset and sadness to my friends and family by me being ill troubled me greatly. I thought I was failing as a Mam to my girls but I couldn't understand it or 'snap out of it'. I thought by being ill I was letting people around me down. It encompassed my whole being.

Once I was in therapy the mental health workers were all very good support but this was short term and basic help only. The sixteen weeks wait for cognitive behaviour therapy when I was severely depressed was far too long. I don't know to this day how I continued day after day struggling with the thoughts and feelings and distress I felt. There were two therapists from the local talking therapies/ mental health team. They were my lifesavers. Both were so kind and patient. The first worked well with me and paced our work appropriately. After the first session I couldn't remember what I had been asked to do at home for the next session two weeks away. She seemed unhappy with my lack of effort but she soon realised that the depression clouded my brain function. I couldn't think straight or remember what had been asked of me. She learned quickly to guide me to write each weeks 'homework' in my notebook as I would easily forget the tasks set for me and she wanted to maximise our time together. She always returned my calls if I was struggling in between sessions. After our second session I rang her during our fortnightly appointments and asked for some literature or books that I could read to fix this problem quickly. I had been ill for five months and was very impatient and unwell with it all. She professionally told me this would take time to heal and that there was no overnight fix. I came off the phone and once again I was in tears at the hopelessness of it all. One of the books she did suggest I had already tried to read but had abandoned it as a result of my poor attention span and memory at this time. In retrospect, I see that I really was ignorant and without a clue how long it would take me to accept all that had happened and be able to live my life without depression being the lead into every day.

    She negotiated extra time with me from her manager once my allocated sessions were finished as she knew I was still struggling with myself. But she knew she could help me and support me into a healthier future if we had a little more time. Her hope and strength turned into my hope and strength and together we learned the true and sincere meaning of perseverance. I will always appreciate her gentleness and the knowledge and skills she used to help me with cognitive behaviour therapy. In some peoples opinions cognitive behaviour therapy is a sticking plaster for mental health issues and I think I am in agreement to this. It just served a purpose of keeping me engaged with mental health support. I still wasn't 'fixed' once my sessions were over.

   I was also supported by a consultant psychiatrist for a short while when my chronic low mood didn't lift sufficiently during the eleven months despite taking around six or seven medications. Then I became very confused as a side effect of the last one. I was agitated and I hardly slept. Once again I lay on the sofa in the sun room, radio on to break the painful silence. I was just waiting for the morning to come. In the morning I didn't feel well and was so disorientated. I couldn't think what clothes I needed for the day or where my clothes were situated in my bedroom. I was not functioning so we went to talk urgently to the doctor. By this time, I had tried every drug given to me. This was about seven antidepressants and I persevered for around six weeks with each one to give it a chance to take effect. Neither me nor the G.P. knew what to do next so an urgent consultation with the psychiatrist was requested by my G.P. - I waited another three weeks to be seen.

   My first visit with the psychiatrist was difficult. I was led to a large room with a desk and two chairs, one on each side of the table. The large room was empty and had a huge window looking onto the beautiful garden. As questions were fired at me and it seemed she spoke too fast and the words were heard but not understood. I wanted to shout out and throw my arms and punch the walls. I wanted to tell her about how ill I felt and how I struggled on a day to day basis to survive but I was so depressed, lethargic and also very British. So I waited. Silently. My head bowed mostly but at times I gazed despondently out of the window. My shoulders slumped down until her talking stopped and I asked her why this had happened to me. I was totally confused, in disbelief of my feelings being so dire. I had greatly enjoyed life before this happened to me.

    She told me maybe there was a genetic element and I had severe treatment resistant depression, coupled with trauma and prescribed me a couple of new drugs. One was a new antidepressant and one an antipsychotic mood stabiliser. She monitored me over a few appointments and as I showed improvement I was discharged after around four visits. It could have been more but I can't exactly recall.

    The whole network of health support and input kept me safe once I was in contact with their systems. I could not have managed this alone. I will always recall all of them and their kindness as I trundled heartbroken through this time with them by my side. I truly believe they kept me away from danger when darkness enveloped my mind. I felt scared for my life and each one of them had belief in my ability to recover and the patience to see me exhibit my beaming smile once more and to witness me once again feel connections that would keep me truly alive.

CHAPTER NINE
MY FAMILY

My parents were always there for me. My Mam listening on the phone for hours trying to help me sort my thoughts out. She told me she had seen it coming and how she saw circumstances becoming difficult at work and the accumulating problems and the unrealistic demands that were being put onto me. I was quite stoical and determined to continue to work. She advised me to take some time off before I actually did. It wasn't until I'd organised everything at work that I made my exit for my own health and actually for the health of my families and clients I cared for. This devastated me. My work was a huge part of my life and identity since the age of seventeen.

During the illness, I did get upset by peoples comments and statements that I heard once I was off work.

'Man up.'

'It's in the past now, leave it.'

'Where's your thick skin?'

'It wasn't your fault' were the ones I heard most. I found this to be very unhelpful and demoralising. A lot of people try to become experts trying to analyse you in their efforts to help and support you. I didn't comprehend if these comments were meant to be well meaning or just people with opinions. Inadvertently, saying this was more damaging.

I was close to both parents. I was so close to my Dad. He was hard working, loving, kind, helpful and had a really fun sense of humour. He adored his family, he supported us all endlessly. We had won the lottery where my Dad was concerned. Poor Dad didn't seem to know what to say but I just knew he was concerned. He still always hugs me when we meet and then also on departing. The hugs were longer, they included a comradely pat on the back then he'd often say 'You ok kid?' He didn't expect an answer I don't think. My answer was always short; I couldn't lie. I often said 'Yeah' or 'I'm not so good' or 'No, not today, it's hard.' I think any more detail wouldn't have been easy for my dad to work with. They knew they couldn't fix me but I think they were with me emotionally. They were always there with open arms if I was near their house and rang to say I was going to call by. Which I often did after appointments. I think they usually liked that. My mum did ask about my darkest feelings. I told her how it was very agitating and frightening because of the depth and blackness of my moods. She asked of the thoughts of suicide but I didn't elaborate. How on earth do you tell the one who brought you into the world that now I wanted out of it. I wanted to be out of the pain and feeling of doom which was torturous every day. I wanted to die. I tried not to burden my parents with this and I talked mostly to the mental health practitioners that came in and out of my life or kept my feelings to myself.

 The disconnection to my children was particularly difficult to deal with as they were young and needed me. My energy was non-existent and my patience waivered too as I tried to deal with their needs and those of a busy household of five people. It is very apparent in retrospect that my feelings for those I loved did stop me from telling them some of my worst thoughts and the feelings associated with the illness.

I honestly thought many times that it would actually kill me. At the time I couldn't quite connect with the anguish the depression probably caused my family but I'm glad that I kept a lot to myself. I felt guilty for regularly thinking of ways I could escape the torment. I had a loving husband and three beautiful daughters. At times this was matterless as the pain and desperation I felt was suffocating me. Yet subconsciously they were my protection.

I don't know some of my family's perception of the illness but I know they were very worried and were always waking me up in the day if I forgot to tell them I was about to sleep. The nights of little sleep and the drugs made sleep an unpreventable and commonplace in most of my days. The strain of seeing me ill was huge for them I now know. I'm sure due to my inferior memory during the illness and afterwards, my parents can recall a lot more difficult or painful things I said at the time but I don't actually recall. I don't talk about it with them as I do with my work colleagues and friends. I think I have burdened them enough.

One of my Aunt and Uncles stopped contacting me when I was ill and I was really hurt as I'd been close to them growing up. I used to babysit my younger cousins often. Mental health issues were never talked about by their generation and they probably didn't know what to say so they stepped back from me. This made me feel rejected and unsupported at a time when I needed to feel loved.

    Yet another Aunt had a lot of time for me and made a patchwork quilt with me for one of my daughters. When I was sewing I felt my mind relaxed for a short time and with a lot of help from her it was a successful project and my daughter loved it. We also used to meet for coffee with my cousin, her daughter, and it was nice to feel quite 'normal' for a short time.

    My family on my Mams side is small and sadly my maternal Grandmother had also suffered emotionally when my mum was a little girl many years earlier. She had hospital respite and my mum was only allowed weekend visits but little else is known. Tragically a few weeks after her mum's discharge from hospital my Grandmother was killed in a car accident. I was sorry to have not had the opportunity to meet her.

    My Grandfather never spoke of her once he remarried and especially as then mental health issues were never discussed. I had always been aware of this and also that my Mam's grandmother had died soon after the death of her daughter due to heartbreak and deterioration of her physical ill health. I am Mam's only daughter and we have no other relatives alive from her family now. So, despite my disconnection to my family, I could see if I carried out my suicide plans it probably would break her heart. She already has a lot of hurt in her memory bank. Sometimes she becomes very fretful and thinks negatively. She's so lovable and kind hearted. She sees her anxious traits herself but she feels she can't change how she feels now. I try to be supportive and a calming influence on her. Once tiredness hit me I couldn't do anything else; I just had to sleep. Mam said how ridiculous it was to sleep so much when I was young and a mother of three precious children. I knew she was right, I was so sleepy; but I could not control it. It controlled me and my days. A deep depression definitely has an awful impact on the immediate family as well as the sufferer. (Note to self: don't think of myself last.)

As therapy went on I did find the sessions very difficult and distressing to deal with. I was often in tears during the sessions and afterwards at home. I tried to tell my husband how I didn't want to fight the pain and torment from the illness every day and I hoped I'd die. This angered him. A selfish idea in his mind. How could I only think of myself when we were life partners and we'd now known each other longer than we hadn't known each other? He continued to work and clean up in the house to keep things ticking over. We didn't have much practical help now that our children were getting older. I say that but if I'd asked my friends or family to help with something they would have probably jumped at the chance. It may have helped them at least feel they were trying to help. The side effect of lethargy from the depression made asking for help in the house near impossible.

My husband did what he could but as a result of him working shift patterns and I often felt very lonely. He was either out at work, sleeping or cleaning and shopping. He isn't a conversationalist at the best of times. He watched me quietly as I suffered every day. He was suffering too and becoming very tired doing all the chores. I just couldn't even attempt to do housework most days or if I did attempt to tackle it I rarely finished it. He, like all of my family, carried emotional baggage and as a result I tried not to say too much when I could keep it in. My husband had tragically, years earlier, found a friend of ours after he'd died by suicide. I was at home the day he returned from work after this happened. My husband's face was grey and full of disbelief and shock. I recalled how it affected him then and how it still does years after. This occurred many years before I was ill. This also left me with so many questions and 'what if's' which remain unanswered to this day. The person is still missed very much. A real loss. A sadness and loss carried by his family in their broken hearts. It takes those left behind often years to come to some understanding in the aftermath of suicide. At that point in our lives we knew little about depression. I thought I did, but I didn't have a real concept or comprehension at all of the confusion and torment that was present before suicide became people's choice. I didn't know that there is sometimes little choice to stay well. I am ashamed to say that after our childhood friend died, I recall thinking that he was very selfish, choosing to take his own life and leaving his children and family and friends grieving and that surely any problem could be sorted out.

Researchers believe that around one hundred and thirty five people are affected to some degree by one persons suicide. (Julie Cerel.2014) This ranges from suicide bereaved-long term, suicide bereaved-short term and suicide affected and suicide exposed.

I was naive and unable to comprehend reasons why some people wouldn't reach out for help. As a result of my experience, I now know many reasons. Firstly, the stigma and embarrassment of having a mental health issue which can be a frightening time for people, too scared to admit as they feel they are failing at life. The lethargy as a result of depression makes you feel that you can't take action to help yourself or maybe having the feeling that there is no one suitable to help. And for some,not having a supportive circle of friends or family that you can trust or open up to and the very long waiting times for counselling and other support services. Through talking to alot of people with mental health issues in my working life, there is often little faith in mental health counselors or a belief that the practitioners don't actually care.

Thankfully, I had no shame speaking out about my health and hopefully my book will step in to reduce the stigma of mental health issues for many. I thought of suicide a hell of alot. I realised that suicide is more complex than a single decision. I believe it is an action taken when an individual feels they have exhausted all options available to them and have no emotional reserves left to fight the pain and turmoil that tortures them. Times of great distress can lead to impulsive actions also. On reflection, the medications also often take weeks to take effect so that depression is then under control of the medication. And some actual side effects of the medication is suicide ideation! I hoped that suicide wasn't my fate but I didnt know whether it was or not. All I know is I felt so incredibly ill, and that for a long time, years in fact, I feared that depression coupled with anxiety and agitation that I experienced would lead me to lose my insight and I wouldn't be able to take anymore. The not knowing was quite disturbing to me but somehow I persevered day after day.

In my worst days I took risks in decisions I was taking and in activities which were potentially dangerous. I played Russian Roulette with my life. I felt I wanted the pain to stop and felt I had little to lose if I didn't make it through the day. I used to leave my home and walk for hours crossing roads without looking or listening for traffic. I would drive my car and chose to close my eyes but then I would think of crashing into other people who were innocent. I heard trains rushing past my town and I knew going to the tracks would certainly be conclusive. I thought of the distress the train driver would suffer. Just like I had when I heard of the baby's murder and experienced complex post traumatic stress disorder. It was a certain way to leave this life full of torment. But did I really want that? I didn't know so I never went to the tracks. After all, some poor soul would have to see the aftermath and that wasn't fair.

    Because I considered many ways to end my life and the sadness of this stays with me still thirteen years later. I was very ill.

CHAPTER TEN
TO THE BRINK

When working in the community, I was welcomed into many homes and met pregnant women and their families on my caseload. I knew my job well. I knew people well. I worked with a lot of other agencies who also tried to protect children alongside me. I worked with some families for weeks, some for the whole pregnancy. I knew women and their cousins, their parents, Grandparents, brothers, sisters, Aunts and Uncles. My work took me deep into communities. Their homes. Their lives. I knew a lot of people. A lot of them were vulnerable as a result of abuse, ill-treatment or living in poverty. A lot of the families were amazing, beautiful, interesting and always unique. They were dedicated to their families and children despite being poor. A lot of them were just great families.

One mother and daughter booked their pregnancies in with me at the same time and their babies were due a week apart by their dates. I carried out double appointments throughout their developing pregnancies at their request. Their babies actually arrived a day apart, the mother delivered first and then was her daughter's birth partner the very next day and saw her grandchild born. It was a very unique situation and quite magical.

I would follow all of my women up at the clinics that I carried out. As the pregnancies progressed I felt as though I knew the pregnant women and their family members well too. Month after month I saw them and monitored their pregnancies and referred them to the hospital if I had concerns. Then I would see them at their homes once they had delivered at the hospital, unless they had chosen a home birth. I attended a few home births in my time as community midwife which was an amazing experience, usually leaving the home afterwards with the family tucked up in bed.

I worked with thousands of families over my thirty seven year career. I must have delivered thousands of babies too but one regret is that I didn't count the number. They were all special in their own unique ways.

My service to the local communities was what made my heart sing. My adoration for and desire to help families through my chosen career as a midwife made what I was affected by all the harder to comprehend and accept.

There had been difficulties and issues there with the new practise manager at the GP surgery I worked at for around two years. She forced a pregnant lady out of the surgery saying she couldn't attend the clinic that I ran. It was because she'd complained that her ill mother had waited too long to see one of the doctors and they got into a heated discussion. This lady missed her antenatal care at the end of her pregnancy as a result of no longer being registered at a G.P practise which appalled me. Sadly, I didn't know this until she had given birth. If the surgery had communicated this to me I would have been able to do a house visit to ensure her and her baby were well at such a crucial time. The awkward manager refused to allow certain blood tests to be done at the surgery. These had previously been done at the hospital even though other surgeries managed to accept this change once it was agreed with the hospital. She was difficult to deal with.

    The conditions around my work had become difficult in the year prior to my illness; larger numbers of families to care for, having the office moved out of town and having to travel an extra hour everyday made lunch breaks shorter and then none existent. Then the G.P. surgery, where I used to have appointments with families, was going to be closed for refurbishment. The surgery manager said she would find me a room to conduct my clinics in, which would be provided by the council. Disappointingly, week after week, time was ticking by and she didn't find me a room. She gave me names to contact people to locate an appropriate room. I discussed this with my management and they questioned why I was having to find a room. It soon seemed that a solution had been found. But the workers in the temporary building were often hostile towards me because I was occupying one of their much needed rooms. I was often moved from one room to another room during my working day. My appointment times were shortened by my manager and the promise of assistance if I needed was promised to me but apparently not to them. Work pressure was increasing with no relief and my manager didn't act on the concerns that I expressed. Maybe she thought my complaints would go away but they didn't.

    A lovely family that I was caring for suffered a still born baby after the uneventful, full pregnancy. It was unexpected and a huge shock to them and myself. A beautiful pregnancy ended with no explanation until tests were carried out. A tragedy. I was devastated by their loss and continued to visit them after the event to try and offer condolences and be a familiar face of support as their life dreams were shattered. I was very saddened by their loss. Me and a colleague were invited to the funeral. It was a cold winter day and we stood shoulder to shoulder as the funeral took place. The memories of that day have never left me. It was such a devastating situation and it broke my heart to witness this lovely family say goodbye to their beloved baby and their future dreams. There were many new safety procedures in place to make antenatal care safe over the years that I worked. Care was planned specifically and appropriate to the individual circumstances once the initial health assessment had been made early in the pregnancy. Although stillborn babies are a low occurrence in the U.K.compared to other undeveloped countries, there is a higher incidence in families of low socioeconomic groups and those with underlying health problems. Poor health was prevalent in the towns where I worked.

PART TWO

CHAPTER ELEVEN
THE FIGHT WITH THE BLACK DOG

I didn't initially refer to the depressive illness that followed as 'the black dog'. I heard the phrase many times and I knew historically that Winston Churchill and Abraham Lincoln had referred to their suffering of mental illness as the 'Black dog '. Isaac Newton suffered from numerous nervous breakdowns and Vincent Van Gogh suffered depressive states coupled with manic episodes and died of suicide. This is not a new illness by any means. It is also not particular in those it captures. Many celebrities have openly discussed their struggles with their mental health; Lady Gaga, Demi Lovato, Robin Williams, Gwyneth Paltow to name a few.

My brain thought constantly while I was ill. No rest. I had a lot to work out. I had intense and continuous distressing and depressive thoughts. One day; I can't recall how long I'd been ill or medicated. Maybe six months. The black dog just appeared in the corner of the room and made total sense to me.

I was home with no pressure from work but I felt the denseness and heavy weight inside of me; coupled with a feeling of despair. I sat still waiting for my next plan or a slight influx of energy to enable me to start another task to pass some time. Sitting quietly. I understood this unfriendly, unwelcomed and often vicious presence as the black dog. He was looking, waiting and he sat there for a very long time. Reminding me I wasn't free at all. I may be home but he was there with me. He had a feeling of total blackness. Sitting. Waiting. I wasn't well. He presented himself as an evil reminder of my illness. I was burdened with awful feelings and thoughts. Like the illness it seemed he had no intention of leaving, he liked my house. He had moved in. No invite, but he had moved in. He and the illness were incongruent, interchangeable. I'd grown to hate them both.

 Well, I watched this black dog. I hated him. He had no right just to turn up here. Days went by. That black dog. Still there. Watching me. Black dog. I was astounded by his persistence. Well I had a choice. I didn't like him. He had to leave. He could not stay.

 I went to my daughter's room as she studied for exams, 'We'll get a dog of our own, that's what we'll do!' I said. It was a childhood dream of hers and her face lit up. Three days later we had a dog. We had chosen carefully and there was a white Bichon Frise in a nearby town ready to leave his mother. A puppy would distract us all from the dreaded black dog that disturbed our peace.

 My G.P. was delighted with my choice and I was quite taken aback by her enthusiasm. I actually thought she would think I was taking too much on. I certainly had not considered the work involved which would be a challenge with my low energy levels. But she explained the calming effect they have when they are stroked and the fresh air I would get as a result of his walks and the responsibility it would teach the children. She was really delighted and at every review I had with her she would remember to ask how I was coping with the dog. He was a cute furball and settled in after a few nights barking and crying for his family. He was great company ; cuddly when I needed it, slept with me when I gave in to it and just the right amount of playfulness. The girls adored him.

He has been an adorable companion and lies at my feet as I write.

We never saw the black dog again.

CHAPTER TWELVE
MY BROTHER

I learned that when depression takes you there is no choice whether it takes you or not. It just encompasses every part of your mind and being. Depression continues to kill people. It definitely has its own agenda. My own agenda had been removed and thrown in the bin. As the months went on and there was no improvement, I no longer gave myself goals or plans other than to attend my appointments and survive each day. My brother had always protected me as a growing child. He was the one with the best paper round in town. The men he sold papers to were loyal and always there every Saturday at six o'clock when the van dropped the papers off outside the closed newspaper shop. Fresh from the printer. The smell of the ink and the smoothness of the paper is a vivid memory still to this day. Money flowed freely and this was before the house calls.The men were kind. My brother was a young entrepreneur. Even when we were younger than this he cared. I remember him rubbing my back through one episode of tonsillitis when a fever had taken a hold of me and I had a rigor. The painful muscle cramps were eased by his massage.

The three of us would jump onto the sofa and watch Saturday night T.V. He had something that was a bit different. No diagnosis. His arm and hand were in normal shape until he was a young boy but as he grew it wasn't as strong as the other and smaller in size. His muscles were weak on his left side. His affected hand would lie softly in mine. I used to stroke his hand and massage it hoping I would help make it better. I used to play with his fingers one by one, bending and stretching them. I patiently exercised his weak hand for long periods of time on a regular basis. I was maybe eight or nine years old. I loved him and felt great compassion for him.

He cared, I know he did.

He, or Dad, used to drive me to college before they went to work every morning. My brother used to come into my room at night when I was a young teenager. I'd watch TV and he'd come to see if I was ok. We chatted about all kinds of things. He would talk of the pool (like snooker but I am not sure of the difference) competitions that he competed in.

As young adults we holidayed abroad together. Me, my husband and my brother. So sweet. So much fun. We would eat together, drink in local bars and sleep it off all day sunbathing. He has a special place with me and always will have.
Sadly the situation changed before I was ill. There were outside factors that negatively influenced our relationship and our relationship became distant. I went to his house to try and understand what was happening; I was left standing on the doorstep, pregnant with my second daughter. For years afterwards at family get-togethers I'd hug him and he'd hug me back and I'd keep the contact open.

I didn't like the friction and the lack of contact after being so close as youngsters.

The surgery that I ran antenatal clinics from for years was opposite his work place and I'd ring him and we'd enjoy lunch together. Our little packed lunches. We'd chatter but the time was never long enough. We always hugged as we departed. I told him he was welcome to our house if he wanted to visit as he was often out and about with his work. He never came but we had some text contact. I never got the explanation for the lack of contact that I hoped for. For around ten years this difficulty was occurring. It was always me making the contact and inviting him to meet. I'm not perfect in my life. I just try my best to be the best person I can be. I thought if I persevered goodness would reign. I didn't contact him for six months when I was first ill as I didn't have a clue what was going on with me. I hadn't seen him around recently for various reasons. On my birthday when he sent his good wishes and I put my heart on my sleeve and decided just to say I wasn't at all well. I didn't get a reply from him. I was disappointed. I understand that some people don't know what to say so say nothing. He was my quiet, kind, wonderful brother. I suppose I hoped that he would recall our love and feel compassion if not for me; maybe for my precious children and my husband who he used to have a good relationship with.

I was honest about my situation as it was, as I understood it. My life was in turmoil and unrecognisable to me. I was unrecognisable to myself. I found it difficult to prepare food, difficult to tolerate it as a result of nausea. No desire to eat. No appetite. I was empty. I'd lost fifteen kilos in weight. I hoped for support and love from him. I was so scared and confused.

    I heard nothing back, no contact; his choice. I will always love him. No one will stop that feeling. It is my feeling. My memories.

    I saw him at a family meal some months later after telling him of my plight. I had recently started a new medication. The side effects of insomnia, shaking hands, stuttering speech were difficult. I'd had a difficult day prior to the meal. My husband said he'd protect me from any difficulties so we went. I was like a snail without my shell that day. I gathered the strength I had and went for my family. I was emotionally very vulnerable and agitated inside from the illness and medication. It became hard to say what were symptoms of the illness and what were side effects of the medication, they intertwined uncannily into one difficult matter. The conversation didn't go well. Despite my state of struggling mind that day I made the decision to self-preserve and leave.

    I had come to the end of being able to be the one making contact or conversation after that day. Maybe he'd changed now after all these years and was not able to feel close as we had when we were younger. I tried not to judge. I felt that I'd offered the olive branch and from then on I needed to save the energy I had on becoming well or healing. At that time I didn't know what path my future would take. I had to worry about getting better; not about anyone or anything else.

He hardly visited or contacted me or my brother. Months went by and no one heard from him. I am a forgiving person as I believe bitterness or stubbornness just eats away inside you if you don't deal with negative feelings.

It wasn't my choice and not in my control any longer. I had enough to cope with and work through. I didn't have any capacity for the hurt I'd carried for years associated with this difficulty, so I let it go. We are still a close family apart from this and love being together; we knew we would welcome him with open arms when he was ready.

CHAPTER THIRTEEN
MAKING PROGRESS

I experienced huge waiting times in the mental health services and I'd say that there are massive gaps where some people fall through without support. I wasn't sure of many things when I was ill. I am sure if I'd been supported emotionally at work and if some of the difficult working conditions had been addressed as the problems were unfolding. If I'd been listened to as I identified potential problems, I may have still become ill but maybe not as severely ill as I did become.

I know it's imperative for the workforce to meet the emotional needs of their workers and it still seems to be a challenge to do this successfully years after my situation. I had no management support in the year I was unable to work. It's such an overpowering illness. It felt like the debilitating downward spiral in my physical health and that the increase in suicidal thoughts would end in my death and this was a secret I carried throughout the illness. Too frightened to share this with anyone.

I was so confused and tortured with awful thoughts and plans to get away from it all. All I really wanted, which my healthy mind now clearly tells me, was clarity and a logical understanding of how I became so ill. I wanted clear thinking and answers to help me understand the illness and to recover from it.

I was always browsing Amazon for self-help books about depression with good reviews. I bought a couple and they mainly were left lying around; partly read and not helping how I felt. Then I read in one book how suicide is a permanent solution to a temporary illness. This hit a chord with me. It resonated through me. Suicide remains to be the only solution in some people's ill and tortured minds but if I could stay focussed I would maybe be safe from myself because I had insight into this awful illness.

I could see that in some people with depression it seemed that an argument, a deteriorating or unstable mood, distress or even a physical illness that seems to go on and on could lead to a personal crisis and leave the affected very vulnerable.

Depression seems to last a long time when you are in the depths of it. It may also appear in episodes but nevertheless it is temporary.

Suicide is not temporary.

I thought about death a lot and in my worst times. I visualised the realness of the people I loved grieving my death and how events in their life may be without me being there with them.

I was trapped. I could not do it to them although I had a real feeling to do it to myself. I hated every suicidal thought. I hated every moment of the illness and every moment of the fight. I hated it so much that I prayed for an escape. I prayed for an escape from the illness and I prayed for God to take my life.

Sometimes the combination of the exhaustion, the severity of the illness and perhaps even the medication caused dreadful black negative thoughts and for myself I just wanted to die. I was so alone and so low that I just wanted to give in to it. I didn't care about dying. I hated living with depression and also the anxiety and edginess that presented. I now know it was probably the new medication causing this side effect of 'suicide ideation' as it's referred to in the patient leaflet. I learned this can be a common thought but thankfully I was too lethargic and despondent to take action and for this I am pleased.

Of course, other people had come into contact with the traumatic incident. The family, neighbours of the family and other health care workers. But I was the only one who had experienced it my way, in my life and with other difficult working conditions coupling up and entangling me in that period of time.

I had a difficult time feeling guilty about and also troubled by these suicidal thoughts and I continued to hide them from those around me. Thankfully I could feel through my black thoughts and eventually I did recall that I had people around me that loved me. My family, my husband, my children, my friends and some colleagues.

I understood the possible misunderstanding and probable anger that would in turn torture them for years to come if I didn't make it through this horrific illness. Eventually, I accepted thoughts of suicide as a side effect of the illness and all it took from me.

I was in such a need for therapy but I had no idea what to expect.

It took a while to even start therapy. Initially, I saw a counsellor related to my job after five weeks but this was very basic and didn't seem to help at all other than me attending an appointment desperate to find answers but neither me or the counsellor knew the answers at this point. I was too distressed and confused to make any sense of it at all. It was twenty weeks before I started standard cognitive behaviour therapy. Twenty weeks that my life was in total chaos. I felt this was a huge flaw in the support services considering how severely depressed and distressed I was on a daily basis. Their workloads must be too big for them too. Just as mine had been.

I imagined that there were too many ill people, vulnerable and unstable people just waiting day after day for their appointment. Ill people. Waiting at home too sick to work. They watch their families leave for the day. They go to work. My neighbours came and went too. They carried on with their daily routines whilst I lost all connection with routine and normal life. The usual daily agenda and need to adhere to plans and commitments disappeared. Prior to being ill, I had always woken up early and dressed early and been fully engaged with life. I used to make the most of every day. I was always proud to take my girls everywhere with me. I liked taking my little ones to the supermarket ready for opening time on the weekends when I was not working. Then we would go to the park and drink juice and have a snack. I used to enjoy full days doing all sorts of things. I took them to dancing for years and took them to soft play with their cousins when they were younger. I taught them to ride their bikes and to skate. I taught them to swim. Nothing was too much for me where my daughters were concerned. Beautiful, busy, full and active days were in my memory cells. Now it was an effort to shower or wash my hair. I wanted to put on my pyjamas after tea. I wanted the days to end. I didn't have any phobia to leave the house but had no energy or motivation to do so a lot of the time. I did always dress but just in whatever I saw first. I hated looking in the mirror. What an awful sight I became. My complexion pale, my sad eyes and facial expression.

I imagine some ill people can't be bothered to connect with others and may have huge difficulties getting to their therapy appointments. It takes a lot of effort to be organised and remember appointments in such difficult times. The mind seems to become chaotic and over busy, over thinking and yet not productive at all. Any cognition becomes a task in itself and a drain on energy. Energy that couldn't be afforded to be ill spent because resources were so small.

I was so desperate to get better so I made sure I attended my appointments. I used to walk to the surgery which took thirty minutes and this sometimes cleared my head of unwanted thoughts. Month after month I waited for improvement. My first therapist was so amazing. In a quiet and compassionate and dedicated way. She was incredible. She was patient but also vigilant. She watched me carefully through sessions and ensured that I wrote my next appointment and homework down and I just knew she would wait and be there for me the next time. I guess I was loyal to cognitive behavioural therapy and my therapist but I couldn't see that at the time. Thankfully loyalty was a part of my character that only flickered throughout the illness. I attended every session with her. Together we would fight and tackle this. Sadly, once her sessions were over I still suffered from depression. I can recall feeling a little better but not significantly so. I understood more about depression and unhelpful thinking patterns but I still struggled with my deep thoughts and distressing feelings.

    About nine months into the illness, one day I felt so depressed and agitated and couldn't stop crying so I rang the doctors' surgery for an urgent appointment and support. This time it was with a doctor who didn't know me. I had hit a brick wall with the medication. It had been changed yet again and it wasn't helping the depression, agitation or the anxiety. I was exhausted and needed some support and to be seen by an expert. I waited in the waiting room, thankfully there were only a handful of people waiting as it was late in the day. My head was down. I hid my sad face from everyone, my reddened eyes; with the darkest of circles underneath. As I sat a mother and baby came through to wait for their appointment and the baby started screaming. I was so absorbed in my sadness that without thinking, my brain triggered and in a flash I thought of the injuries the murdered baby had sustained and I imagined how the baby would have cried helplessly as it was hurt. I started crying again as I was called into the doctor. She was obviously surprised to see me crying. I said the crying baby had triggered me and she sarcastically said 'Well that's difficult for a midwife.' Due to having depression I couldn't be bothered to explain. I obviously knew I was in a difficult situation. I wasn't working at that time, all I could hope was that I'd improve enough to work again one day. I knew it wouldn't be any day soon. I didn't feel supported at that appointment and I went home feeling very scared about how easily I was triggered and once again how very lost I felt. I did learn to talk myself through the triggers sometimes but the whole process and reaction was exhausting. I think friends and family probably found this the most difficult part of the illness; despite antidepressants I continued to trigger and experience visualisations of the injuries and torture that was caused to the baby before it died as the manager had escribed to me.

   I needed to get back to work. I knew that during my eleven months of sick leave I was unable to work as I was so ill but then I became fearful of losing the career that I loved . No one suggested this would be the case but I needed to make a move to see if I would once again be capable of my job. It was agreed that I was to do office work for a couple of months. I wasn't ready to put my professional mask on and deal with the public quite yet and all the demands of my midwifery role.

    Looking back I still wasn't well at this point but it gave me a routine and I felt included in the workplace once again. I had regular meetings with my manager and soon the months were ticking by. It was said to me many times though from professionals working with me; the occupational health doctor and my G.P. that 'it won't be plain sailing', or to 'take baby steps.' The lovely occupational health doctor who had supported me in my illness, said most employees with severe mental health issues wouldn't attempt to get back to work and in fact eight out of ten didn't make it back. But slowly I seemed to steadily move forward and manage all that I was expected to at work. After around eighteen months of trying to manage work, I thought that I was feeling better in my mood. I discussed a plan with my G.P. to come off the antidepressants. I felt they were making me lethargic and causing nightmares so I wanted a break from them. About ten days after what I thought was weaning myself off them I became suddenly very ill. I ended up being blue-lighted by ambulance to accident and emergency with severe abdominal pain and chest pain and breathing difficulties requiring a morphine painkiller 'oramorph' and entonox (gas and air) to relieve the pain. As I waited in the wheelchair in a queue of ambulance workers and patients, unable to stand, the manager who had not supported me in the aftermath of the murder passed me as I struggled to sit up in the chair. She acknowledged me but didn't stop to talk to me and in that moment I felt let down once again and I was filled with hatred for her. It was thought by the medical staff to be pancreatitis but turned out to be a withdrawal syndrome. I was dizzy, nauseous and in a lot of pain; it was agony but they couldn't help me. The accident and emergency department had offered little guidance. There was nothing that they could do so I was discharged. On the drive home my husband had to stop the car as I vomited at the roadside. This and the other states I found myself in when struggling with depression, was so humiliating. I arrived home with an anti-sickness and antacid to try.

    I visited the G.P. the next day as I was still feeling very ill. I couldn't eat, I couldn't walk without being doubled over because of the pain. The only way to stop the problem was, the G.P. told me, to restart the antidepressants. I really didn't want to so I persevered for three days and nights with the debilitating withdrawal effects hoping it would ease at some point. But I couldn't manage any longer so three days later I decided to restart them and luckily the withdrawal symptoms eased almost immediately.

    Once the symptoms settled after a few more weeks I still felt ready to wean off even with the risk of those awful side effects. But ended up medicated on specialist medication from the psychiatrist after I relapsed once again.

CHAPTER FOURTEEN
FIGHT OR FLIGHT

The depression still didn't lift in the first year. My brain was on high alert to a danger that no longer existed; a feeling to flee or a sense of impending doom which felt as though it would kill me. An internal trauma. Agitation and distress ruled my mind and this was very difficult to cope with. It became obvious that I was showing signs of post traumatic stress disorder now.

I shouted out and screamed at night more than previously and my poor husband put up with it all and took hold of my hand every time. He often complained at the time but was never really cross about the disturbances, but he too was often really tired from our sleepless nights. He was more patient than I was when he persistently snored in the early stages of the illness. It was hard waking regularly in the night and hearing his bear-like snoring and knowing at that point he would be hard to wake if I needed him. I told him how lonely I felt and that was why the hand holding started so I felt less alone and it surprisingly worked. During the day, loud traffic noise or being amongst a lot of people agitated me and sudden noises often triggered me to be prepared for the 'fight or flight' physiological response. I often flew into a rage and was irritable with the family too as a result of complex post traumatic stress symptoms. Complex post traumatic stress disorder developed due to me not witnessing the murder but knowing details of the injuries before the death and it traumatising my brain.

The agitation of post traumatic stress disorder was often severe. My brain felt threatened by internal danger regularly. Like the time I'd travelled to London. 1987. I travelled alone to visit my now husband. That night I had to navigate through the underground as a young eighteen year old. I was in the newsagent buying a drink and a few of us heard an explosion. 'A bomb?' People shouted. I grabbed my bag and quickly walked into the underground towards the direction that I needed. I had always previously planned the journey with my fiance. This night he was working. It was the first time I had to navigate the underground alone. As I continued to walk, people were running towards me. I walked quicker. I focussed on my planned journey and not to deviate from that. Then the threat of danger set in. Fight or flight. There were too many people to get through. Their faces expressed pure danger. Agitation. Fear. Initially, I couldn't work out what was happening. The world turned silent as hundreds of people ran towards me.

It was the night of the Kings Cross fire. I was suddenly crowded by people panicking so this sent me into a fright/ flight response to run from what they'd seen. I ran for my life. I ran into the streets of London. Smoke pouring from the entrances to the underground. Ambulances, fire engines and police appeared everywhere in no time. Confusion, panic, fear, death. A tragic night killing thirty one people.

I wasn't deep enough in the underground to be trapped. I was free and physically unharmed. As I ran through the streets of London looking for a taxi to take me to my friend's house, I saw another girl running and she was frightened too so we ran together. All the phone boxes were changed to 999 calls only so we couldn't ring for a taxi so we ran until we found a taxi office. No one we knew had mobile phones in 1987. We stayed together till our taxis arrived and took us back into our separate lives and thankfully into safety. It did bring a feeling of confusion, disbelief and a few nights of disturbed sleep but no more than this.

During post traumatic stress disorder, the fright and flight feeling was internal this time but felt the same as seeing the external fear and feeling the threat to my safety during the night of the King's Cross fire. I was quite aware that there was now no external danger but my mind felt and acted the same. The agitation became so bad that sometimes I couldn't sit still. I would sit in one seat and immediately want to change rooms. I would go to my bedroom and feel terribly lonely. I would leave the house but want to come home. Sometimes it felt so bad I did think my mind would take control and I'd lose all perspective and hurt myself.

I often felt unsafe when I was outside next to the traffic incase I made a hasty move to hurt myself. These were the times when I really did think that I'd do something to physically harm myself to release the pain. I took a knife out of the kitchen cupboard on a few occasions and took it to my wrist. I imagined the harm I could cause myself as I held the knife to my skin. After a few minutes or so my thoughts started to register and I was once again saved by the love for my daughters. How would I explain to them why I had cut myself? The answer sounded lame. To release pain? I knew the pain of the illness still wouldn't leave me so I put the knife away.

    I considered self harm many times but I'd force myself to pay attention to 'now'. The times I wanted to not feel anything anymore. I would try and shift the focus onto what it actually was I was feeling. I would face it and concentrate on my surroundings very specifically. It saved me many times. I would often leave the house briskly when I was struggling with my feelings. I would walk and listen to the wind or any birds or traffic noise. I would try to make myself take note of anything that was happening to know the moment was real. Even if I felt something only slightly pleasant for a small moment I would recognise that it did feel nice.

    I used music a lot too as a distraction when I was walking; U2, Coldplay, Prince, Genesis, Queen, Hozier, Florence and the Machine were some of my favourites. I often played music so loud on my headphones to drown out my repeated thoughts. As I focussed on the lyrics sometimes I did start to feel better as I walked. Sometimes if I couldn't override my thoughts and ruminated unintentionally, I would end up once again crying as I walked. It was unpredictable how a walk would end up; helping or not. The feeling that I needed to flee my home continued to happen regularly throughout the illness.

I kept myself safe when I was with my dog as I wouldn't want him hurt or frightened if he saw me hurt. He was good company and I felt I should protect him and not frighten him or allow him to get hurt.

At home, when the pain was extreme I couldn't manage to shift the focus onto positives. I hated it. I considered a lot of possibilities to avoid staying in the pain of the moment. Anything to avoid the pain. I would sleep, or sit motionless curled up with my knees bent up to my chest and hugging my legs tightly to feel safe.

In the early days, especially in the first year when I was on waiting lists to see therapists, I struggled a lot and I retreated to my room and took diazepam to sedate myself for a few hours and give myself a break and respite. Then, I could make a promise to myself to try again in the morning. I was frightened to do this regularly. Frightened of becoming addicted to it or thinking it was not good to avoid the problem itself. I didn't want my daughters to know I was using sedatives but it saw me through some very desperate moments. It kept me safe in the way that I was actually rendered helpless for a good few hours and it would eradicate my harmful thoughts. It was prescribed by the doctor and she trusted me to be safe with it. I was still quite aware that I would still have a battle on my hands in the morning but at least I'd have had some sleep and there was a slim chance of new or clearer thoughts the next day.

When my thoughts were painful, which was every day at some point in the day or even the whole day for a number of years. I noticed that the pain didn't ease but sometimes it didn't worsen either. I would try so many ways just to get through it or get through the next hour. I felt burdened and a physically 'heavy' sensation or a denseness in my head which is too hard to describe. I also had tight knots in my stomach continually which at the depth of my illness stopped me eating very much at all.

When my mind was torturing me I was restless and nothing much really helped. I could meet a friend or go to my parents' house but I still felt ill and anxious. There might have been a moment where we had a hug and I felt loved but it was only a very short moment in the day. I was alone a lot of the time, the children at school and my husband working or busy in the house.

Walking was often my way to pass time and get through the next half hour in the day. I would just go and sit outside somewhere near my home. There's some big sandstone boulders nearby; blocking an unused road. Coat tucked under me and fastened tight; that is when I remembered to put it on as I often left hastily without it. I would sit there and try to think of nothing. I often left in the dark and there are also rocks nearby and they are not visible from the road so I would sit there and feel invisible and hide from my thoughts. I would stop fighting with myself and when I thought I could bear the cold weather no more I would make myself sit longer. I learned to let whatever thoughts come and then go. My painful and black thoughts. I would sit and wait. This was maybe the medication starting to relax me. I didn't know but I recall a definite lessening of the agitation when I sat and waited. Once I was outside, I often didn't want to go far away. I felt the safest I could at home. One day my little dog wouldn't walk and I gave up trying and so I just sat in the middle of the path beside him. I later discussed it with my therapist and she praised me for going with it and not fighting that moment. I knew it would look strange to any passer-by. I didn't look around. My head down. Stroking my dog. I didn't care anymore about what anyone else thought of me. They didn't know my story. Staying with the moment or mindfulness is something I read about when I was ill. The book is still unfinished but I read some of it to understand the concept. Reading was hard to focus on and recall clearly. I still forget a lot of the content but I manage. It is interesting to re-read books after some time anyway. It made me realise that although time is moving on very slowly nothing would dramatically change in a small moment. Unless I did hurt myself. I tried to believe that although the depression was lasting way longer than I firstly thought it would, one day it would eventually leave me just as long as I kept myself safe.

  To onlookers so much time had passed but in my mind it still lived with me every day. It was as if I was trapped in time. My nice G.P. explained how time was fluid and forever moving but this was very hard for me to see or comprehend at that time. As the months passed by I thought the worst of the depression must be nearly over. Once again I was ignorant of how long a severe depression and the aftermath of a trauma could last.

After a number of years I was referred again for further therapy. The second therapist sensitively guided me through the trauma therapy. It was called EMDR (eye movement desensitisation reprocessing.) Initially we talked about my history and thoughts around it and I broke down. After the first two sessions I left the room and felt broken. I was so distressed after speaking of the very raw feelings that I still experienced. I sat on the step outside the clinic in the rain, uncontrollably sobbing. I hoped someone in the offices by the entrance would hear me and alert my therapist to help me. No one came. Exhausted, I left for home. In one therapist session I bravely skirted around my very negative thoughts and she listened. I said 'I know you understand what I'm going through because you've helped so many people deal with different traumas.'

'No I don't understand what you feel; you are the only person that has experienced this in your life. I don't know how it feels.' she replied.

My heart sank. I desperately needed someone to understand me. I felt only the G.P understood me and my visits were fortnightly and I felt this was not enough support in the acuteness of the illness.

Three years since the incident, almost to the actual day, I realised that I was actually still very alone.

The eye movement desensitization and reprocessing therapy (EMDR) did help eventually after a number of weekly sessions. Staying focussed on the therapy when the memories were so raw was extremely difficult but I felt I needed to go through the therapy in order to move on. The therapist started to ground me during my distress which arose frequently as we did the treatment. I sobbed through the therapy but she encouraged me to face the visualisations that I suffered and the trauma and pain that triggered me regularly. We identified what my triggers were and focussed on them during the treatment as she moved the object backwards and forwards past my eyes. She explained that it was similar to rapid eye movement during sleep with processed thoughts. She fearlessly worked with me giving me acknowledgement and hopefully a way out of the repeated torment. I did feel that the treatment helped but I was surprised when the depression still didn't lift. I was better from the point of triggering with complex post traumatic stress disorder but still very anxious and confused as to why this should be the case. As our sessions came to an end she revisited my thoughts of suicide and she asked if I felt that way would I ask for help.

I said 'No' the three times she asked. She underlined it three times on her notepad. I knew she would do nothing. I was so exhausted from being depressed and at times I lost hope and this was one of those times. I had expected to be healed after EMDR and felt going through the trauma and sobbing through treatment hadn't helped as much as I wanted it to. I knew myself well by now and how determined I could be, not all the time, but I had it in me to not survive the depressive episode. This concerned me as it was evident that I wasn't 'fixed' yet. I had more healing to do despite EMDR coming to an end and with no plan in place, no scope for further appointments. It also stopped me from reaching out to counsellors or professionals as I struggled on for years as I felt I couldn't be helped. Medication kept the severity of the depression and anxiety at bay a lot of the time but not all of the time.

Being ill impacted on all relationships. Some people, work colleagues and some friends couldn't stay in contact and ride the storm with me. Once I had confided in them I just didn't hear from them again. A couple of my close family regularly met with me and texted and called round to see me. Meeting them helped develop some structure and slight sense of purpose while I was living with depression. I made plans to meet them and rarely changed plans. I tried to keep contact with people open instead of isolating myself. Sometimes I managed to make meetings happen, but at times I felt I was very alone even in company. Fighting the depression took a braveness I hadn't ever needed prior to this illness. It was the toughest time in my whole life.

Then, meetings in public started to bring social anxiety with agitation and tension that I wasn't used to. I managed to talk but often stuttered and had trouble thinking of words I needed. Half the time I didn't feel coherent at all. Particularly my work friends who had retired, were so kind and compassionate; if they thought anything derogatory toward me none of them said so. I was just uncomfortable being me at that point anyway and I didnt want to be judged. They never made me feel awkward or unduly uncomfortable and their support was priceless.

CHAPTER FIFTEEN
FRIENDSHIPS

There were some friendships that continued to go well during my illness and some which failed. There were friends who enjoyed the good times prior to my illness. Some of the good time friends withdrew from me as I could give nothing as a friend.

The illness was eating me up inside. I was also empty of emotion apart from sadness and doom. I had nothing inside and they turned away. It was a shame. It wasn't me withdrawing from friends. It was the illness making me sink to a very dark place and dragging me right under. I had to fight to salvage any normality in my life. It's incomprehensible to most that it's depression that chooses the way forward for a time, not the sufferer.

Obviously life isn't all roses and sunny days and sadness and disappointments do sometimes reign as a result of some people's choices; over which I had little control while I was depressed. I had the rest of my life to hope some difficult situations will heal and improve some relationships. There were friends that couldn't ride the storm alongside me. I did feel abandoned by a few people. A couple of friends I confided in and I never heard from them again. I had to accept their choices. After all, I knew I was often terrible company to be with.

Throughout the depression nice things happened too but any feeling of 'niceness' was very fleeting. I felt unwell every day. I felt burdened and pained inside but could go out with my friends or meet them for coffee some days. I mostly stayed afloat during the conversations. If there were more than two people with me I did struggle to follow the conversation. If it was too noisy I'd suffer head pains and agitation and want to go home. If I was too tired or very low sometimes I didn't always bother going. No one made the agenda but me. A number of colleagues I had worked with and not socialised with much before my illness astounded me with their thoughtfulness and kindness.

 Very special relationships developed over the years that I was ill. They made me feel cared for with texts and meetings to have coffee. My experience of support, particularly by friends and work friends, was mostly good and I was very grateful for their care.

 When I knew my mind was ill and I was diagnosed with severe depression I started to see patterns in my behaviour. At times, I would withdraw from people at times I needed to reach out for more support and help. There was one colleague who I would message for support, especially when I feared not making it back to work. Her and her husband were so very supportive in their responses to me. I needed to see what they saw in my future and abilities.

 Did I still have what it took to be a good midwife? Their compassion and support was so massive and consistent over the months that I struggled. This contact was extremely valuable and their faith in me recovering really helped me as I really respect them and their opinions. It felt like my identity was lost while I was incapable of work as it had previously been such a big part of who I was. One lovely midwife friend used to come and give me regular reflexology; week after week. It would be during the evening when the house was quiet. I would be dressed in my pyjamas as she worked her magic as I laid down on my sofa. It was very relaxing and she listened patiently as I tried to verbalise my chaotic thoughts as they went round and round in my head.

Another lovely friend used to text me, pick me up from my house and we'd go different places for walks. One day we went to a nature reserve or bird sanctuary or something. I hadn't been there before. It was a cold day; maybe February or March. We were dressed appropriately for the British weather on this day, which was just as well. The wind from the north was bitter cold. My legs were freezing as we walked. My cheeks were rosy with the chilling wind. We walked through a wooded area and came to a small lake. It was sheltered and the wind no longer blew against us. The sun broke through the clouds and glistened beautifully across the calm water through the bare trees. We stood there and I really felt the beauty of the moment. I wanted to stay there. Away from my life, my difficulties and most of all my thoughts. She stayed with me by the water watching it glisten and we listened to the birds sing. She said nothing; she didn't need to. She was there for me in the early stages and if I wanted a chat or a walk years on from the onset of my deterioration she was there. This friend was patient and kind. She was thoughtful and throughout the illness she persistently checked in on me to see that I was ok. She never finished my sentences or rushed me no matter how much I struggled with my words and my thoughts.

I think the onset of the illness had taken her by surprise because we worked together and she'd been aware of the difficulties building up against me. I had expressed my angst and we had tried different things to help improve things. But I just kept struggling through the daily battles which would present themselves to me.

I made sure I told her when I was recovering and I saw her when I was back at work how much of a good help she'd been. She isn't usually a tactile person but I got a hug that day when I told her how much I'd appreciated her hanging in there with me. She demanded nothing in return. It can't have been easy for her seeing me in this deteriorated and depressed state. My mood was up and down for years and she stayed in touch throughout my worst times. Sadly, we did lose touch after a number of years but then I contacted her and it was just like old times and we enjoyed our walks once again.
I have a few other very close friends. One is like a sister to me. We have poured out our feelings to one another hundreds of times over the years. For a long while she did more listening than talking. She knew exactly how I was doing because she has been the closest and most constant support.

Her kettle was always on and her arms open to me; particularly after therapy sessions.

She would know when we were shopping together if I became anxious or agitated. She would know if I just needed to go home.

She never appeared to tire of being there for me. One day she asked if she'd upset me because I'd been distant for a couple of weeks. This was about ten months into the illness, I can't remember exactly. I didn't even have the energy to write anything for my book at certain times during the illness; only when I had periods of improvement I wrote.

This lack of memory is very strange to me but actually also very useful that I don't recall a lot of my difficult or awkward behaviour.

I had become distant because I thought I'd been in the lowest mood possible and then for a reason I don't know, it worsened and I really segregated myself from normal life and any activity associated with it. I couldn't be bothered to meet friends now. I'd been ill for what felt like a very long time. I was actually just going through the motions of pretending that I was participating in my healing process. I felt that I couldn't do it anymore. My emotional energy was rock bottom. I was exhausted. This resulted in my G.P referring me to the consultant psychiatrist with treatment resistant suicidal depression.

Support is a very protective factor in people suffering depression, my doctor said. I had a lot of people around me but it wasn't protecting me anymore. I cried in my dear friend's arms; devastated that I'd hurt her. She cried because I had been in such a state for such a long time and she'd misread the detachment. I was just trying to cope and protect her from my dark thoughts. I often talked repeatedly about the circumstances which lead me to be ill because I didn't understand why I became ill. But for once I had nothing to even say about my illness anymore. Nothing else could surprise me about how awful it felt. I now know I was at the very lowest point; such a lower and darker place than I'd ever thought possible. But it was real. I was in a massive black hole. There was not even a flicker of light at the top of the hole. Not even the equivalent of a tiny candle flickering. Nothing. It was totally black where I'd plummeted to.

I willingly increased the medication and prepared for the side effects once again. I curled up like a baby and slept in the day, an insomniac by night.Now my detachment had affected my closest and dearest friend in my life. My most discreet and lovely life buddy was hurt and very concerned that I was stepping back from her. I think I did it because my mood and thoughts were so awful that I didn't want her to know what I felt inside at that time. Isolation was a significant feeling that I often felt when I suffered from depression. I felt it even when I had support or was actually with a group of people.

I realise this was incomprehensible to most. Occasionally I received cards and letters through the post from midwives that I'd worked with over the years in the community. It was positive to have people sending a note to say they were thinking of me and the family and saying I was a miss in their life. At the time of being suffocated by the depression I had no comprehension of how this was helping me. I also didn't feel happy about all of this attention. The words in the cards often said 'enjoy your family time.' I really didn't get this because I had difficulty connecting to the children at times. I was detached from all positive emotion. It was kind of my colleagues to show they cared but I often used to consider dressing and making myself presentable to see any of them too much of an exhausting chore. The lethargy from the medication or the insomnia made everything such a task. I had jeans and a favourite jumper which turned into my security jumper. My 'blankie.' I had two; a black one and a pale turquoise one. I thought people couldn't tell if my jeans were clean or not so I didn't care if they were clean or dirty. My hair was often tied up and oily. I couldn't even deal with washing it often. I couldn't be bothered and didn't care what anyone thought. I'd wash it before it was too oily. My self care was poor. They never commented. They were kind.

    One day I had a real surprise visitor. It was one of the G.P.'s that I'd worked alongside at the surgery for ten years. My team leader from the community had frequently visited me and through our numerous conversations I had come to realise this wasn't going to be a short illness, although I still didn't understand how long it would be until I actually started to improve. At some point I came to the conclusion that I couldn't go back to the surgery. I told the team leader to let the doctors at the practice know I wouldn't be coming back. The G.P came with a beautiful bunch of flowers for me and a card in which all the doctors and nurses from the surgery had written in. I was really touched by their thoughtfulness. They were sad to see me go, they said. After all the difficulties certainly hadn't come from them.

    I had less energy resources than prior to the illness. I needed to salvage my life purpose and that took a lot of doing. It took a lot of time, patience and energy.

I learned to look after myself and I no longer ignore my body or mind trying to let me know I'm under stress or exhausted, or over worked and I made sure I had meal breaks at work which hadn't always been happening.

    I decided to no longer tolerate unkind or hurtful people or those that don't bother to check in with me. I love the friends and family that support me unconditionally. They are very special people and I won't let go of those ones.

CHAPTER SIXTEEN
FAR AWAY FROM HOME

   I recall another good friend, a midwife who I had known for over twenty five years; having met when we first started our careers. We had our children together and we always confided in each other. She is trustworthy, kind and empathetic. We live thirty miles from each other now but this didn't stop her from keeping in touch and telephoning or texting nearly every day.
   As I lived through the depression everyday life continued month after month. It was time for our annual family holiday abroad. There is an expectation that this should be a happy time with no other worries. Realistically it was difficult in that I slept poorly in the new surroundings and I got agitated easily. Often, I walked alone for hours around the places we stayed just passing the time. I also listened to music via headphones a lot, which drove my buddy who was holidaying with us, crazy. I had tried my best to be cheerful in front of all of our children and thought I hid my depression well. My holiday photos that year are awful for me to look at. I looked so lost and sad.
   My friend that stayed at home would take my 'facetime' call every morning or so when I rang from the poolside. I called her regularly around eight o'clock as I was feeling alone and homesick. Once awake I couldn't stay in bed where my thoughts would ruminate. No one from our group of two families woke so early. She never became tired

of helping me. This was such a lifeline for me. She was a very good friend.

It's hard for a lot of people to imagine feeling unhappy in a beautiful holiday setting and perfect weather. It didn't fix anything for me. The depression, post traumatic stress and anxiety persisted. I didn't even enjoy clothes shopping beforehand as people may have expected. I especially didn't enjoy packing the clothes sufficient for five of us as my brain functioned so chaotically.

On another annual holiday, I was again, with my family and my friend and her family. I can recall lying at the beach with some of them, I recall my husband wasn't on the beach at that time, Just me and my friend and some of our children. We dipped in and out of the vast blue sea with the children as we became too hot from the summer sun. I was lying quite relaxed lying on the beach, for once my thoughts were quiet.

I was suddenly triggered by a baby who started crying. I didn't have time to consciously think about the situation. I instantly was triggered by the thoughts and knowledge that I had about the injuries of the murdered baby. I cried and pretended to our kids that I had sun cream in my eye as I tried to wipe the silent tears away. But they kept coming. I was so very angry with myself and I hated myself and my reaction. I was very annoyed at being ill for so long. I had struggled with depression on and off for five years up to this point. The details of the baby's injuries before its death, shared by my manager and the G.P. practice manager where I worked was greatly damaging to my mind. I was trying my best to behave normally and have a break on a holiday. Everyone around me was fine; only I heard the baby it seemed. I looked for the baby but couldn't see the source of the noise past the bright sunlight. The intrusive images of the murdered baby's injuries infused my mind rapidly. The tears flowed and I furiously got up and rushed across the hot sand to the sea. I saw no one. I just focussed on the sea. I was full of hatred towards myself and the illness. I was exhausted by it all. I waded in and left the world behind me. When the water became too deep to walk I swam. I swam sobbing. I swam out to sea until the beach was a blur. I was so angry at the constant interruptions to my life. It affected me continuously. There was no peace and no reprieve. I got angrier and angrier as I thought of the many times I'd trigger so instantly and of the times I struggled with my low mood. The symptoms just went on and on. I treaded water.

The area was silent. I could hear no noise now. Only my own cries. Once again I was totally alone. No one from our families had followed me. So I treaded water and thought of ending my life to end the pain.

I desperately needed the pain to end. As I bobbed about far from the beach I wondered how many hours I could stay there before I would die. I hated myself and I definitely had no self respect for triggering in these ways. I also didn't care about myself any more. I only cared about my beautiful children but my distress was so great at this time that I didn't think of them at this moment. I tried to exhaust myself as I continued to tread water. I put my head under the water numerous times hoping my body would just disappear from the world and I would be dead. Disappointedly I floated back to the surface, I was so very very sad. As I came up to the surface the salt water stung my eyes. I wiped them with my salty hands which didn't help at all.

Time blurred as I stayed in the water in my dire state. Suddenly, my attention was drawn to a shoal of angel fish which swam past me and touched my feet and lower legs. Usually I wouldn't have liked them touching me but I was taken back by their colours and stripes and their majestic moves. I watched in amazement at seeing something so beautiful as they swam by. And as quick as I triggered into the distress I came out of it and decided I shouldn't die. I swam, emotionally drained, back to the beach ready to engage with my girls once again.

CHAPTER SEVENTEEN
THE CHILDREN

Midlife often brings a greater maturity and comprehension of life itself being created with time. The new understanding of midlife can be empowering as the work/life balance changes and eases allowing more free time. I was enjoying the challenge of managing well over a hundred families a year on my part time hours when I worked on the community caseload. I was a community midwife for ten years.

My children have always been my priority and I was always happy in my work choices. I always tried to remember to work to live and not live to only work but I enjoyed my chosen profession a great deal. I watched people a lot during the depression (that didn't take too much out of me.) People going through their days so briskly and precisely and repeatedly.

I saw my neighbours with their little children. I have lovely neighbours. They were going fast too though. They took their little people to childcare, nursery or school. I wonder what they made of all this speed. We have all done it; wake the children early to clean them, feed them and dress them before taking them to their place for the day until our work is finished.

There is pressure of schedules and time, clock watching. It doesn't matter if the parents or little children don't feel like rushing their breakfasts after climbing out of their warm beds or being lifted out of their safe warm cots. Little people don't have a choice, now I know that ill people don't either. Day after day I saw the speed of life in the people around me. I had little else to do. So fast the people moved. So slow my days went. So painfully slow. No change in my mind-set, and no improvement in my mood. I was so disconnected from normal life. How on earth did this happen?

I have loved children all of my life. I babysat from the age of twelve years for a lovely family who I'm still very close to forty years later. I always wanted to be a mother and was very patient and thought I was born to be a mum. I was the best Mam I could be but there were many stressful days and pressures to juggle home life and shift work as most families have these days. The noise from three lively, healthy girls and often visiting friends, was incredible! We managed and had a lot of good times with a handful of difficulties thrown in.
Then the illness came.

My precious children lost the Mam they knew for around five years. My memory is sometimes kind and makes me forget some of the finer details and I'm now very grateful for this. I was not grateful for what appears to be black holes in my cognition. It was very frustrating being lost for words or jumbling words up so that my words come out wrongly or as two combined words in one. Fortunately, it caused great amusement in my girls!

I cared for them the best I could during the depression. I had no interest in eating and certainly had no enthusiasm to cook a healthy meal for them. My husband is our chef thankfully but I really struggled when he wasn't home. My weight loss was partly as a result of medication side effects making me feel sick or nauseous and partly because I ate so little. The other factor was psychological; I didn't want to live so why eat. They are good children and as they became older they often made my food which I greatly appreciated. At first tears used to stream down my face at the kitchen table when we all sat down. The children silently looked at me and each other. Their Dad was out working and their Mam home but not at all 'with' them.They often had hugs for me but often they were angry with me too. There was a lot of silence. A lot of sad faces; not just mine. I just couldn't break free though. Seeing them sad as well and knowing I had no energy to be the very best I could be for them. That broke me. I would keep my tears in sometimes and break down and go in the shower to sob. I hoped they wouldn't hear my cries. I learned in therapy that this was teaching them that I thought it was wrong to cry in front of people. It felt that it was best when it released itself. Many times it really did. I couldn't stop it. I was bereft.

 I dreaded the children asking me to take them places, to go shopping or asking for friends to sleep over. I had no energy to manage the days; never mind adding more activity of any sort to it. I tried to hide the feeling of dread on my face. But they knew I didn't want to do these things. I couldn't face the noise or crowds at the shopping centre. We struggled through for a long time.

They saw me sleep a lot in the day because of my insomnia at night. I'd sleep anywhere. The sofa, the bed, the children's beds, the floor. I didn't care. When I needed sleep I couldn't make it wait until an appropriate or family convenient moment. At my worst and blackest times I did not appreciate the love for my children.

On reflection, I have always loved them and always will. I have built my life around the needs of my children, providing for them, staying home, and rarely going out, just so I was there with them. I only left them with family or friends if I did go out or worked when my husband worked.

Severe depression detached me from life as I knew it. I wasn't as loving and didn't connect with them as well as before. This is a very hard thing for me to comprehend now and was even harder then. I hid this from everyone. Even my trusted therapist and doctor. The guilt was awful and still isn't great. Unless you've been so ill I think this is too difficult for anyone to understand. Of course I see now that children are our future and life's miracles. They are quite resilient in many ways and we somehow survived together. They are very caring and perceptive of others feelings; whether this is a result of what they've experienced or genetics I will never know.

This was very difficult for me to write, to permanently make a note, knowing one day they may read this.

I was in the mental health support system and would attend all appointments in an attempt to help myself. But, during the nights especially, I struggled. I struggled alone. I had visions of my death, what actions would lead to my death and also of my funeral. I fought these thoughts off. I visualised my children at my funeral. I feel terrible guilt over even having these thoughts.

At my worst and blackest times I really believed the illness would ultimately kill me. I thought a lot about this. Thankfully, I always had the insight that it wouldn't do the children any good if I escaped the trap I was in by suicide. Even though I often couldn't feel my love for them because of the illness I recalled that they are my most important people in the world. Such agonising thoughts created turmoil and chaos in my mind.

I understood that I had to suffer this illness to reach a positive future with them. I changed from bed to sofa most nights. I concentrated best I could on the radio. The irrelevance of what was being said annoyed me but it helped as it gave me a sense of time and to observe the slow and painful shift towards dawn. I hoped my feelings may lessen and have a different depth that I could cope with. There was no schedule at night. Time was slower, no agenda; only survival and keeping a sane perspective and a vigilance to call for help if my actions became hasty or dangerous.

I always considered others first before myself. This altruism and my precious children were my safety net. My children will recall how at random times in the night I would join one of them in their bed. I would always just say that I needed a cuddle. They always obliged and shuffled across the bed so I could cradle them. Usually in the fetal position, we would curl together. The realness of their breathing made me concentrate on them. My mind would distract and settle. I gently smelled their beautiful skin and hair. I lay still. Careful not to disturb them. That wouldn't be fair. They were probably at school the next day so it wasn't right to disturb them.

    Silently I cuddled into them. I was being. Being with my children. In the still of the night.The purpose of my life in my arms. My precious children.

    I was petrified of myself and my own potential to devastate their lives if I made a wrong move. Forever vigilant, I lay with them. I stayed as long as they would allow or until I felt exhausted. I then returned to my bed or the couch. I had always protected them but now they were protecting me. They made me safe despite the chaos I felt within myself.

LOVE

I don't love & I don't care
The person I see here or there
Without love the mind is dead.

My child, her eyes they glisten
Her mouth smiles
Her voice giggles
Our eyes meet, I love, and I melt.

I love, I melt, but my heart remains broken
She persists, she cares and gives love
Love so deep and sincere, it's meant to stay
My Angel child, she knows no despair

The rose grows, its petals unfold and
I place it in her hair
Our hands hold onto each other
It's simple, its love, purest of all
My love can't be taken
I hold tight; reliving that small moment Over
and over again.

I do love her and she needs me to care
I lie beside her in the cold night
Praying to see night change to daylight
I wait and I wonder and fear our fate
A tear of love; she needs me near
The torment of being ill

It's a taste of life without love

I have love, I have hope
I care; now I feel love.
I will stay.

PART THREE

CHAPTER EIGHTEEN
LISTEN TO ME

The early therapy was challenging but the therapist was always with me to guide me and support me. Some sessions were more tiring and confusing than others. Sometimes I couldn't concentrate, it was a struggle to even comprehend what she was saying. Despite her gentle and knowledgeable mind I was often confused. One session, we somehow reached the core of the situation.

The talk of the baby murder was a brave move we made together. I thought that I was ready to talk about it. I had often wondered how the subject would be approached or ever find its way into my therapist's carefully guided sessions. I had often feared the moment which was now upon me. It had to happen. I needed to say it out loud. I needed to give myself a chance of healing and recovering from this situation. I recalled it to my therapist all as if it had happened the day before - it was actually eighteen months after the day that I'd fallen to my knees.

Pain and emotional turmoil had stayed with me since I had seen the television news report that announced the murder. Children's murders seemed, in my ill mind, to be common incidents. Gruesome acts and injuries caused to innocent babies or children. Sometimes there seemed to be news reports for consecutive weeks on separate children being harmed nationwide. As an adult and mother and midwife these incidents catch my attention. Sometimes I switch the news off in an effort to protect my precious children. They don't need to know of the cruelness in the world. They are young and innocent.

A big part of my job was trying to protect children. Now I had a situation never known to me before in my thirty year career; an untoward and unpredicted act of violence against one of the babies I had tried to care for and protect. I had admired and cuddled this baby. It was the biggest blow my work had ever delivered to me. Countless people told me to remember that it wasn't me who had harmed this baby. In my mind this didn't matter to me.

The pain I felt was crucifying me. It dug deep into my soul. I felt abdominal pains as I couldn't stomach what had happened. I couldn't comprehend who would have done this. As we talked, the feeling of sharp pain in my abdomen started. This was recognisable. The pain which had tortured me since hearing of the death. Perhaps it was my body expressing the pain that my mind was suffering. It felt like a burning poker being stabbed into me; into my raw painful wounded body. I began to wretch. My arms wrapped tightly around my waist giving counter pressure in a loose thought that this would ease the pain. She watched as I precariously made my way to the sink weeping. I couldn't stand straight; doubled up with pain. I think my intention was either to vomit or to put my head under the cold tap, or maybe both.

I sobbed uncontrollably. The distress was no longer suppressed inside of my body. I had been so reluctant to face the pain; it had been trapped inside for a very long time. Since the day I'd been told, by a manager, of the exact injuries the baby had suffered, I had refused to repeat it or talk in detail about it. I couldn't risk increasing the pain I was already experiencing. In refusing to talk, I felt that I was also protecting the person trying to support me. Over time, I realised it wouldn't damage them as it did me. They didn't know the family or the baby and never would.

She suggested that we cut the session short as I wept, concern for me written all over her face. 'No, No, we must do this' I said courageously. We continued. We had fifteen minutes left until the session ended. Time in therapy was precious. I had been told I had a limited number of sessions allocated to me and I wouldn't see her for another two weeks. But she was right to call it a day; it took me time to straighten my thoughts and recover from the issues we addressed.

I left the session. Quietly, with my head to the ground. I can't imagine how I looked. I started walking home. I usually walked to and from therapy. A way to process some thoughts. Time to be outside and make my body exercise. I wasn't eating due to the abdominal tension and pain and the depressive mood. I'd lost so much weight and was the thinnest I'd been in my adult life; even compared to when I was a long distance runner. This day I would struggle to stay standing on my thirty minute walk home. I felt disorientated. Totally drained; I thought I might collapse. I walked with heavy legs. I staggered and burst into tears once again. I lost all concept of time. Time played tricks on me these days.

    I kept my head down and kept trying to move forward. The hill in front of me looked like a mountain. I thought of my options. I could have changed my route to avoid the steep hill but that would make the walk longer or I could have telephoned my husband to collect me. I would gain the lift home but lose my time to work out what was happening to me. I couldn't face either his questioning or him telling me he wouldn't allow me back to therapy as it obviously was making me worse in his opinion. I tried to walk on. About five minutes later I could go no further. Too far from home and no one around I knew to ask for help.
It was another of my lowest, saddest and loneliest moments. I attempted to grasp at any logic in all of this.But were we making some progress?
We had to be?' I questioned.

    I was very alone. I looked around in desperation. It was a cold day near the end of the year. The day was dull. The wind was icy and it was drizzling. I crossed the road and walked into the church yard. Surely no one here would turn me away. I walked to the door. Locked. My heart sank. I couldn't walk home.

I turned and saw the place I'd spend the next hour or so. A seat at the side of the graves. I remember the seat was wet. Raining heavily now. I slumped down into the bench within the stone walled graveyard. I sat still. There was no one around. I thought of the therapy session. The stomach pain was still as severe. I let it all come out. Sobbing and sobbing. The pain. The sadness. The loneliness and the many questions.
Did I miss anything doing my job with this family?
Why could none of us prevent it?
What led up to the murder?
Why oh why?
Was it my fault?
I repeatedly recalled the months of care. I questioned myself, had I missed anything?
Was I one hundred percent sure I hadn't missed any signs and that I had perceived everything correctly?

I had to be sure. My mind was in chaos. I could only get through this if I thought if I was sure. It was always very sad dealing with baby loss and I did my best as a professional supporting clients after such awful incidents. But little babies and children shouldn't die. I knew it happened but It shouldn't. It was incredibly sad and upset me terribly. Being an empath, I never found it ever became any easier.

The difference was this was murder. A baby had been tortured and died. A little person I knew and aimed to protect via my work. I cared about all my clients. I loved to have an excuse for a cuddle off a little person or baby. This one was no different. The confusion around the murder was to last. It was nearly two years before the culprit would be identified and imprisoned.

I sat alone, so very alone. My thoughts of why I was depressed became clearer, but the thoughts didn't lighten. I didn't have an answer or a way forward out of the severe depression. I didn't recognise myself or anything about me. I sobbed and prayed as I sat on the church bench. I was so afraid that I would not heal. I was so isolated and so very alone. I prayed. Quietly. I prayed. I begged God for help.

I had always believed but rarely prayed until I was ill. Higher powers than us had to exist. After all, are we mere mortals with no right to understand the world? I prayed and asked for direction out of this, I asked in my prayer for a 'friend' to help me. I didn't know how to find one of my friends who worked in the area. Where were they all? I was no longer a community midwife and no longer had no work phone with all their contact numbers in. That was taken back alongside my kit bag as I was replaced by another midwife once it was known that I wouldn't work back in that area of work.

Their lives were continuing at such a fast pace. I felt left behind. No longer capable of working or even getting up in the morning to get to an adjusted role or alternative job. For the first time in my life I was actually incapable of working and functioning as a regular human being. I was just surviving day to day.

I prayed to God for help.

I so desperately needed to be loved and have a purpose in life. I needed to recover from my emotional distress. I didn't feel my life was worth anything anymore. I felt nothing but pain and negativity. I really needed a hug. Someone to put their arms around me. Someone to hold me and take away the pain for one short moment. My thoughts eventually emptied. I had none left. My body was so very cold. I'm sure I could feel the cold nearing my bones. The cold was attacking me, my jeans were soaked through. My coat had reached its saturation point. Rain was seeping slowly through it around the neckline and the shoulder seams. I had to make a move. No one had come to help me. I saw no one. Before I moved on, I visualised myself unconscious in the cold on the grave yard grass. It wasn't an option. That would frighten someone. So, I stood up. I had to get home. I left the grounds and as I stepped onto the path there was my friend! It was a co-worker, my colleague, my friend from work. She didn't usually work in this area but there she was! She was great to work with but we didn't usually contact each other outside of work but she had sent me a lovely worded card a few months into the illness. She was over the road though and about to knock on a clients' door. I had begged for a friend to help so I had to let her know I was there. She was looking the other way. I shouted her name.

    She heard me and looked. She focussed and she made her excuses to the client as the door was opened. She came out of their driveway towards me. She was shocked to see the state of me, I could tell without hesitation. She held me close and rocked me and made me feel safe. I had been crying for probably an hour and I cried again now. She said a few kind words and her compassion and strength poured onto me.

I knew she had to go back to work. Time was so tight these days for NHS workers, so I couldn't delay her. Prior to this we had a good working relationship and mutual respect but at that moment a connection was made that was very special to us both. It remains with me to this day. It was a very poignant moment in the illness. Realisation and acknowledgement of the awful state I was in by both of us. She told me that she thought I was recovering and was shocked to see me so distressed.

I walked on and rang my husband. 'Please come for me; I'm a bit upset today.' He arrived within minutes to take me home. He listened to me that day. He didn't say much, he rarely has deep and meaningful conversations. He's just a quiet man. The doctor increased the medication to smother the pain at my request. But I had my therapist and I had a suspicion things wouldn't stay like this forever. Outside of my despair, time was moving forward and my thoughts had been acknowledged and heard. That day I was definitely 'listened to.' I had Faith.

CHAPTER NINETEEN
COURT

For months I was told I wouldn't have to stand in the dock in court. I was relieved to know this and it helped me through the acuteness of the depression believing this. The authorities had my statement and I was told that I wouldn't have to attend as I was still affected by illness as a result of the situation. Then a phone call came from the police with the court date. In six weeks' time I would speak the oath and answer to the judge and the prosecutor and whoever else I had to. I had never experienced the British judicial system. I was in for a huge shock.

I was so frightened that in my fragile state that I would answer their numerous questions incorrectly or that they'd twist what I said or I wouldn't know the answer. I was frightened of the possible reactions that I could have. I thought that I'd freeze and look foolish or even cry. My mind was still not strong and my memory poor; it was going to be a struggle to even remember what had been asked of me. I was truly petrified.

I had a new manager at work and she tried to get a medical exemption for me so that I wouldn't be put through the strain. It wasn't possible to avoid it. I did attend. I had a pre court visit with a colleague and we took turns standing in the witness box. I practised the oath having only previously heard it on television before. I read it out loud and my vision blurred. Once again I cried. The stress was incredible.

I made myself read it out louder so I would be sure to know how loud to read it on the day. My new boss, who had stood by me since my return to work, had insisted to the courts that she would be with me on the visit. She also insisted that she needed to be allowed to sit inside the courtroom on the day I'd attend.

I had been back to work for a few months when the week of the hearing arrived. We were scheduled into the court on the second day of proceedings. I wasn't driving much then because of the side effects of the antidepressants. So I took the bus and would walk ten to fifteen minutes to the court. I could cope with that and the short walk may straighten my mind. I hoped. As I turned the corner I took a wrong turn leading me on an alternative route. I wasn't too concerned and thought it led to the same area. What I hadn't realised was that it was a much longer route and only realised this when I met my boss at the entrance and she was frantic to my whereabouts. I had no concept of time. My phone was on silent and I didn't realise it was getting late and we were just in time to be allowed inside. Little did we know, once our bags were checked by security that we would wait six and half hours for my time in the witness stand. We sat in a small room. About ten of us were going to give evidence. They were mainly co-workers from the surgery. We weren't allowed to talk to each other about the case. The wait was long but the court staff were helpful. The lovely lady that had shown us round on our pre visit looked after us all day. A few people who went to the courtroom before me. We watched as they returned to collect their coats silently and leave. Everyone was incredibly nervous. We tried to read their expressions as they briefly returned to collect belongings. Desperate to leave, they gave nothing away.

Then I was collected. My boss and I were taken to wait outside the courtroom. I faced the huge, engraved wooden doors and stood silently. We waited an unknown length of time; until they had finished questioning the previous witness, I assumed. Whilst waiting, I walked away from the doors and distracted myself by looking out of the window and at photos on the wall of historical criminals from the 1800 and 1900's. I concentrated on keeping myself calm.

Since finding out about the murdered baby this was the worst day of my life.

The previous witness was escorted from the court by the ushers and taken away. Then more ushers appeared and explained there was to be a temporary delay. It was the end of the day and two witnesses from another part of the country were complaining that they were to enter the courtroom after me. We found out that they weren't prepared to wait until the next day and have to stay away from their homes and busy jobs.

I was aghast as I was taken back to the small room; stressed and shocked by the decision to make me wait longer.

A wait that was again an unknown length of time, and may now result in me waiting until the next day. I started panicking, thinking that I couldn't deal with waiting another night.

Thankfully the judge wanted to see me before they closed the court down for the day. I don't know whose decision that was but I was very grateful for it. Again, I stood outside the huge engraved wooden doors waiting for them to open and to be escorted in. I was told by the usher that the court had been told how this murder had adversely affected me. I had no direct evidence and did not know who the perpetrator was at this time. My new manager sat immediately behind me in case I needed to ask for time out to compose myself or have her support. Crown Court is a very expensive business so we had to come up with a very brief time out strategy. In the moment I was able to focus and I didn't need to ask for time out. They seemed to be very kind to me. I read the oath clearly but was indeed told to speak louder. I knew I had to address the judge directly with the answers but I felt I had to look at the person asking me the questions who was at a different side of the court to the judge. I needed to be sure I'd heard the questions correctly. In crown court great respect is expected when addressing the judge. Once it was known who the judge was we had been briefed on the day to say either 'Sir/M'Lord /M'Lady after each

question. It sounded bizarre and old fashioned and didn't roll off my tongue easily. Afterwards I was told I hadn't needed to say it after every single question!
It was embarrassing as well as difficult and uncomfortable but I couldn't risk being chastised in court. Especially as I was already so very fragile.
I was told afterwards that I could have held onto the wooden stand. It would have certainly helped steady me.The adrenaline had raced around my body and made one of my knees weak and I had to transfer my weight from leg to leg to stay standing. My boss had been sure I was going to collapse because of all my movement she could see from behind me and she did not know what I was doing.
I answered all that was asked of me and we left. My boss offered to take me to the bus station or home. I declined her offer and walked back to the bus station not wanting to put her out of her way.
The next week was a blur. The stress had wobbled me once again and I sunk back into a severe depression. I took a week's leave from work and retreated for a short break away from home to avoid possible damning newspaper reports of the case and of the devastated family's response that no one prevented the death. No one could have prevented this death. Only the person who was found guilty and imprisoned could have prevented the death and it certainly wasn't a health care worker. Even though someone was imprisoned after that court case for a long time, there was and remains to be no reprieve or relief from the effect

this had and still has on me. A baby died and I'd worked over twenty years to prevent such situations arising. I wasn't guilty of anything but the effects of the shock and trauma will stay with me forever.

CHAPTER TWENTY
MOVING ON

Over a year after having my mental health breakdown I went to work clinically. I changed my place of work and I said I was fit to work and it was agreed with my occupational health department (who were great once they started seeing me regularly) with adjustments to my work. Court was over and the correct person was imprisoned so I thought that justice had healed me enough to move on.

I would have a phased return to clinical practice and be exempt from twelve hour shifts. Instead I would continue, after my phase in on seven and a half hours days.

I had fought against severe depression and post traumatic stress disorder and now I psyched myself up to fight for my job and livelihood. My G.P and new manager were so supportive and knowing that this support was now in place was vital in helping me cope with my return. I saw my new manager, the occupational health doctor and human resource colleague frequently and was provided with coaching support too. As a result I started taking little steps forward.

It was decided that I would no longer work on my own caseload and I would work back in the hospital. My area of work was to be the labour ward delivering babies and caring for the women who were being induced or planned caesareans or those who were very ill with complications of pregnancy as well as labouring women and deliveries. I felt working one to one with women was where I needed to be. It took a lot of concentration to do my job well and it often distracted me from myself and my struggles.

I became a functioning depressive. I grappled with my mental health issues and started to accomplish day to day tasks and uphold my responsibilities of being a mother and midwife once again.

I had shorter working relationships with clients in my current role. I now had the strength and desire to be a supportive and positive member of the team, whilst hiding my depressive symptoms. Being a supportive colleague made a difference to helping my colleagues manage their work in a cheerful environment and perhaps it would brighten their day too.

As I cared for work clients and colleagues I also started to care about myself again. I started to look after myself and I protected myself. Thankfully I didn't forget my job or how to care about people. That was a huge relief as it's the only professional passion I've known. The need to open my heart and allow caring to be part of my working life again was one of the biggest hurdles I overcame on my return to work.

My words resounded from a therapy session where I'd asked myself 'How can I go back and sit by the fire when I was burned so badly? How can I care again and go back to a job that hurt me so much?'

But I did it. I did care again and the passion for the job was in me, once again, as it was before. I once again believed that I could improve the experiences that clients had by having a positive and pleasant attitude. And by providing good standard care obviously too. I felt brighter at times and it also helped make days easier to manage. I treat the women, their families and my colleagues with kindness and respect.

In my recovery, once I was back at work, I was able to empathise with work colleagues more as a result of my struggles and guide them in obtaining help and support. Now that I feel stable and have a deeper understanding of how awful mental illness is and how valuable kindness and appropriate support and listening to someone is.

As time passed by I thought that if I needed support again that I would take actions to ensure I get it. I won't take complacent answers. I would ensure that I looked after my own health and I hoped to stay healthy and have a positive energy which I know would have a ripple effect towards others. I was the perfect eccedentesiast. I don't remember my first day back, my first month or even the first year. All I know is that I succeeded and continued to take antidepressants and mood stabilisers to assist me in staying in the best emotional state I could possibly be. I worked four shifts a week as I had in the community, partly to prove to myself that I could still function as a midwife as I had done for many years. There was a lot of support around me to help me work in the busy environment. My new colleagues were supportive and patient with me as I often talked about what happened. I was still in shock about the situation and how ill I'd become.

Then after around two years of being back at work and three years after the start of the depression, I had a very unusual case to deal with. A new colleague had started at the labour ward and she was so upbeat and great to work with and we became good friends. She called me at 5am to say her son's girlfriend, whose baby had been induced because of health reasons, was in the hospital having contractions and would I come in for my shift and look after her. She said that she was struggling to manage the pain. I showered and psyched myself up for the shift ahead. I attended the room and immediately saw the concern of my colleague and her son as his girlfriend laboured and moaned with pain despite already having an opiate injection. She wasn't very coherent and it was the first time I'd met my colleagues' family so I introduced myself first. In some ways it was business as usual, as I made the necessary observations required in my role. She progressed really well in her labour and was soon ready to push her baby out but there were concerns over the baby's heart rate. I suggested she move onto all fours position to aid descent of the baby and this might speed up the delivery as the pelvis is thirty percent bigger in this position. Indeed the delivery was quick. As the baby was born I handed the baby through her legs and sat the new-born up against the back of the bed and the mother lifted her to her chest. Me and my friend, now a Grandmother, dried and stimulated the new baby to the beautiful sound of her first cries. All was well as the new mother cradled her new-born. We sighed a breath of relief and wrapped her in warm towels and my friends' son cut the umbilical cord. It was a beautiful birth and I felt honoured to be a part of this. We took photos and it was a very special time. I have a black and white copy of the photographs that we took. It was one of my favourite photos. Me in my uniform, a beaming smile and laughing eyes. I treasure the photo I have of me cuddling the baby. I just felt elated. We were all delighted that the situation turned out to be fine and the baby was beautiful. I, in fact, felt this was a pivotal time in my return to work. I felt proud of myself and this was something I hadn't felt in a very long time as my self esteem was suffocated by the depression.

There were many births, natural, instrumental, caesareans and my shifts went by quickly and time started to move on. My colleagues were supportive and I aimed to support them in return. I talked a lot to my friends and colleagues and maybe for them it was difficult to repeatedly listen. They never gave that impression and were kind and appeared to listen. I have never hidden what happened to me and have always spoken openly and honestly about it. My understanding of this repeatedly talking was that I was unravelling the confusion connected to how I became so severely ill and how this and the event actually shocked me into suffering a severe, life threatening persistent depression and PTSD.

At times my mood wasn't great and I struggled to wear that professional mask portraying that all is well. On reflection, I feel my mood was quite flat despite being medicated for years. Often I just wanted my shift to end and to go home. Often I felt exhausted after the emotional or physical demands of my work but I persevered and time did move on without me realising it.

I still felt trapped by the historic events and the past repeatedly came into play in my present life; there was no escape. I often thought I hid this well, but whether it was really hidden from my colleagues I don't know. I ensured that it was definitely hidden from the families I worked with as I wouldn't have wanted them to perceive my low mood and I made sure it didn't have any effect on the care I gave. The concentration required to do my job safely helped me distract from my depression but also it was overwhelming some days and I coped with this by sitting quietly once I was home and reflecting on my situation and my day at work.

I always felt that I could message my colleagues, who were also my friends, if I had worries or concerns after my shifts, they are very supportive to this day. This helped me process thoughts from different viewpoints and helped me to be the best practitioner that I can be everyday that I went to work. I was making progress but I couldn't always see it.

When I had symptoms of depression, I would withdraw from family and friends and felt no one cared about what I was going through and the regular battles I still had. It also felt that I'd never been free of depression and I would forget good moods/days or nice times with family or friends.

CHAPTER TWENTY ONE
THE TRIP

    Time passed by and my daughter asked me to take her to an Ariana Grande concert and I felt that I couldn't cope with planning and travelling at that time due to my anxiety and depression. It felt as though it was too much pressure for me to deal with that. So when the opportunity came around again a few years later and I was coping better with life, I booked tickets for the concert in Manchester for us both to go and enjoy. I booked the train journey and hotel for the night after the concert to make a little break for us. The journey after my work was fine and we were really looking forward to seeing the performance. The train arrived on time and as we stepped out of the station we saw the Arena next door. It was a trouble free and very manageable journey but our first visit to the city so we decided to go straight into the Arena to find our seats and wait for the start of the show. The performance was brilliant and we enjoyed the songs, the music, the dancing and the great buzzing atmosphere. My daughter looked so happy. There were young people dancing in the aisles and people just having a great time around us.

    At other concerts, I have sometimes left before the end to avoid the rush of the crowds when I needed to retrieve my car and drive home. This night, there was no rush as we had to find our hotel after the show. The last song was over and that's when everything changed.

    We were still at our seats when the bomb exploded in the foyer. It was so loud and for a moment everyone was silenced. It was easy to know which direction the noise had come from and where we had to avoid.

    Moments later, screaming started from all directions and panic set in inside the Arena. Some people appeared to freeze and others fled. I wanted to keep calm for my daughter and I promised her that I would get her out safely and asked her to hold onto my hand. She was fifteen years old and I felt overwhelmed by the need to protect her. The difficulty for me at this stage was not knowing if we would actually get out safely and whether there were other bombs or dangers in our path whichever way we chose to leave. As we turned to leave at the nearest exit we saw empty seats with bags, coats and shoes having been left behind from those that had fled for safety. There were people running down the stairs towards us at the bottom. There were also people jumping over the safety barriers and fleeing.

    Once we were outside we had no idea where our hotel was. We had been so excited to go to the concert we had stepped off the train straight into the concert. We were running away outside. I hoped we were leaving the danger behind but I didn't know whether this was the case. Total fear set in when we asked a policewoman which way to go to leave the town. She looked panicked and just waved us away, 'Just get out of town' she said so we ran on.

We found a taxi rank with a long, still queue of taxis. I knocked on the window to ask the taxi driver to take us to our Hotel. He told us they had been instructed to stay still and not drive.

I was really stressed at this stage, I held tightly onto my daughter, I felt we were like moving targets not knowing if there were any more bombs. I started to get stressed and panicky and realised we needed to stop for a moment. We took a turn into a side street car park and we hid crouching down so I could catch my breath.

My daughter quickly put the hotel address on her phone map and we set off to find it. We had a feeling that maybe the danger was behind us after running quite a way. We walked and as we turned a corner there were two girls and one was obviously having a panic attack and her sister was trying to help her. I crouched down and started talking to the girls and told them to come to the Hotel with us and to phone their Mam and tell her what had happened, that they were with an adult and ask to be collected from the hotel. Onwards we walked, the four of us, as we reached the bar in the Hotel I asked for cold drinks and we sat down in disbelief of what had happened. My daughter was talking to my youngest brother on the phone when the staff member told us we had to leave the Hotel as the Police had said it wasn't safe. He's always been close to my girls and been so supportive.

The girls were collected and went home and once again my daughter and I were in the streets of a strange City feeling that we were moving targets and may come across another bomb at any time. We walked quickly through the streets, trying to make my daughter feel safe but in hindsight we were both very frightened. I made a plan to book into the nearest Hotel no matter what it cost as we needed to feel safe inside somewhere. We were devastated the next day to hear the extent of the atrocity and deaths caused by the bomb. It was absolutely devastating to us both as we headed to the train station to come home. My close friend was a welcome sight on my return as she was concerned about our welfare. She wasn't wrong to be concerned as it triggered PTSD symptoms in me once again. I spent the next few weeks and months trying to come to terms with what happened that night. Shortly afterwards I wanted to show continued memory for the twenty two terror victims and chose to have a Manchester bee tattooed on the inside of my left wrist; my only tattoo.

CHAPTER TWENTY TWO
DAD

I managed work for a couple of years and I wanted to have more free time to work on my health. I reduced my working days to three days from four. I remained medicated. I occasionally felt well enough to reduce my medication under the supervision of the G.P. The medication wears off slowly so has to be reduced at intervals to avoid the withdrawal effect. Every time I reduced my dose symptoms of depression would return. So I ended up staying medicated.

After five years since the onset of depression and of being on and off medication a great blow came to our family; my dad collapsed. He was rushed to hospital and after head scans we were shown that he'd had a massive brain haemorrhage deep in the right side of his brain. He was semi-conscious as he lay on a trolley in the assessment room of the stroke unit. He could follow some instructions and point to his face with his right hand but his left side was totally dense and immobile. His smile crooked, his expression sorrowful. He couldn't talk to us but he looked at my Mam and mouthed 'Sorry.' He was always so very thoughtful. He was a healthy man prior to this. He used to drive the campervan around Europe from Spring to late Summer. They used to disappear for months on end. The morning of the collapse he was in the garden and must have started to feel unwell. He went to the window of the bungalow and knocked for Mam and said he was falling. Mam rushed out to him to find him collapsed on the path. She rang my young brother who lives the closest to them and also for an ambulance.

The effect of the brain haemorrhage was life changing for the whole family but particularly for my parents. The hospital staff told us that they didn't think he would survive.

He literally couldn't do anything unaided. His swallow reflex was absent for a few days but then he improved slightly and he was allowed thickened liquids. When he was allowed to eat, his first choice was ice cream!

He was hoisted to a special supportive chair, he had no feeling in the left side of his body. He had a lot of physio in the hospital to help him learn to sit straight without pulling to his helpless left side. He was really frustrated and exhausted, sleeping a lot of the time. Over time his speech did return thankfully and when he had learned to sit again he was transferred to the hospital I worked at for rehabilitation. He worked hard everyday and my Mam was by his side learning how to help him. He was so tired and slept for hours on end which worried Mam as she just wanted him to keep practising everything so that he would heal. She thought it was time wasted when he slept, she wanted to hurry on his recovery. My brother and I were by her side as much as we could around our work and family commitments. At this stage Mam didn't want my older brother contacted, she had enough to deal with and didn't feel it was the right time as we hadn't seen him for a while.

My younger brother had recently moved to a new place of work so although he couldn't take time off he managed to keep going to work and then to visit the hospital. When I was off work, I was with my parents too.

One day my brother was at work and my older brother walked past him which was bizarre as he didn't know where my brother's new place of work was and or that he'd moved his place of work. So my brother thought it was a sign and he should know. He told him what had happened to Dad and once again we were all back in touch with one another. I would message him with any news or changes with my Dad and he always replied and came visiting every week to the hospital. After a number of weeks of intense therapy, Dad was discharged home with a standing frame as he couldn't safely stand without full support. The change in him was devastating to us all. He needed assistance with everything. Getting out of bed, showering, dressing, eating, standing; the list was endless. My young brother and Mam worked closely together as it was physically demanding for her petite stature in comparison to my dad who was taller. I helped dad with as much as I could when I was there. Praising him for his efforts and pointing out the small improvements. He used to get annoyed with my Mam's persistence to make him exercise, but over the months it paid off. His left side became stronger and with more rehabilitation at home, he learned to walk with a zimmer frame and then a walking stick. Gradually he became strong enough to walk small distances with the walking stick and his wheelchair was needed less. Mam worked on his strength on his left side and the dexterity of his left hand and eventually he was able to get some use of it.

   He was slowly progressing but still needed a lot of support from us all. The next spring they bought a luxury static caravan near the river. Dad could manage the four steps up to the door and he felt relaxed and free in there. Mam managed Dad better up there and he started walking without his stick for a few steps. At the end of the year they had just come home from the caravan when one afternoon when I was due to look after Dad and mam rang to say he wasn't right and he was confused. I rushed over to find Dad was really confused. He was looking right past me and trying repeatedly to get up out of his chair. He was very agitated so I explained he wasn't well and we needed to stay still until the ambulance crew came to check him. It reminded me of when I was a young nurse and people I looked after had dementia or delirium and I learned to talk to them calmly and quietly and gain their trust in order to care for them and ensure they were safe. I checked his blood pressure as we waited and Mam had checked his strength on both sides and it seemed to be the same as usual with his left sided weakness, but he wasn't right. The ambulance crew arrived and were thorough with their checks and didn't think he had another stroke but he was unwell enough to be seen at the local emergency care centre. He was very confused. We reiterated he wasn't well and needed to be assessed. Once seen by the ambulance crew, he was blue- lighted back to the stroke unit at the regional hospital for specialist care. We were told after scans that this time he'd had a clot/stroke on the opposite side of his brain; it was twenty months after the first haemorrhage. We were devastated once again, he'd had such a nice year at the caravan. He seemed only slightly affected this time but when we looked at the scan it was a large clot and we couldn't believe he wasn't badly affected. This time he was transferred to our local hospital after a few short days and we couldn't believe our luck with how he was only affected a little but he seemed forgetful and tired. The familiar staff welcomed him back to the ward and he started physiotherapy once again. My Dad kept his sense of humour this time and put all his effort into his exercises and slept in between his sessions and meals. He was nearly ready for discharge home when one morning he was walking with the physiotherapist and he collapsed again. It was only five days after his first clot. This time Dad was severely affected and exhausted as he once again lay helpless in the bed. It was an emotionally difficult week but we pulled together as a family to be near him. This time it was difficult to stay positive as the outcome appeared severe and my parents had already been through so much. I was by their sides as much as I could at the hospital but I was feeling the strain. It broke my heart to know he had more to battle through. My Mam was badly affected seeing Dad was in hospital; it saddened me greatly.

Dad lay in the bed and our future with him was unknown. I had been trying to manage on a lower dose of my medication but I could feel my mood plummeting. I couldn't get an appointment with my G.P. at this time. I had talked to him a month earlier. He said I could increase the dose of the night medicine that I took to stabilize my mood and help me sleep if I started to struggle. I was just about keeping myself afloat at that time. I tried to keep on the low dose but I began to feel emotionally exhausted and I once again surrendered and increased my dose which usually stopped any symptoms of depression. I had to take a week off from work and decision making in order to rebalance myself.

Day by day my dad started to improve once again. He's definitely a fighter. I believe he recovered from the strokes and the haemorrhage because he was a fit man in the first place. We soon had him home and although his sight and hearing seemed permanently affected and he seemed weaker when he was walking, he was in good spirits and glad to be home.

My brother and I visited as much as possible to support Mam as it took a toll on her, and she became brighter as a result. My older brother visited a couple of times too and we are all happy to have him in our lives once again.

    When we're not working I meet my older brother for a walk and coffee in the local park and I feel so happy to see him. We chat incessantly as if we've never been apart and I'm delighted for this outcome after a difficult number of years without him. I have put this upset behind me to focus on the future time I have with my brothers and family.

CHAPTER TWENTY THREE
THESE DAYS

Months and years passed. There was no light bulb moment, there was no pattern to the good days that somehow appeared, my flat mood just changed and before I'd realised I'd had whole weeks of descent days with minimal low mood. On reflection I was severely depressed for around five years. Nothing significant had happened, I was just slowly making my way through the fog. I had further episodes of depression totalling thirteen years. I was in and out of counselling and G.P. support but this was progress. Although it was intermittent, it was definite progress. Sometimes I felt well and coped with all that life had in store for me and my family and other times I was worried and anxious with a low mood.

It's cathartic for me to write and it sets things clearly in my mind; writing, editing and rewriting. It also gauges how far I have healed and this makes it possible to write it without the raw emotion that would have previously made this an impossible task. It was pertinent to write it though in an effort to help and guide someone else from despair into a better future.

I started to feel light and unburdened and happy. Once again I was experiencing fun and laughter with my children, I felt like an excited child as butterflies passed fleetingly through my stomach. There was no longer a feeling of doom or the heaviness I used to feel.

I became extremely self aware and definitely more experienced and knowledgeable about depression and all that it was. My G.P. practice were excellent at supporting me when the need arose. I learned to deal quickly with myself if the black mood reoccurred. I also had the combination of medication and the exact dose of them which was therapeutic to me. I hoped that I wouldn't have another total breakdown as severe as I have experienced. But I didn't know whether I would. Every few months, with the same medicines I started to feel really good and I believed that I could come off them but have never managed to. But that's okay. I had concerns with the medication I take as it had risks of weight gain, heart disease and diabetes developing and I wanted to avoid these illnesses as much as I could as I have always looked after my physical health. Recently, I swapped the mood stabiliser for a lower risk one which was an achievement. Frustratingly, over the years when I reduced the anti depressants I would seem fine initially and then my mood would plummet. Then I would feel fearful of another mental crisis so I would increase the dose but this would take weeks to take effect and I would struggle and once again lose my confidence and self esteem. I would feel that I had to hide behind a mask especially at work in order to cope with demands of work and provide good quality care and support to those in my care.

    I had regular support from my G.P. practice and when my mood deteriorated or I needed to discuss my concerns I could always get immediate help. Exercise has always been recommended by my doctor as a form of self-help. So I joined a gym to see if I could lose some weight. I gained twenty kgs with taking the medication over the years. I had no choice though. Many of the medicines that I initially tried had negative side effects so I stayed with the ones that kept me most stable but resulted in weight gain. Once again my perseverance is tested as I hope week after week to have lost weight.

   Two years ago I restarted the 'couch to five kilometre' running app, after a seven year break from running. My daughter and I managed the nine week programme and successfully managed the runs but we didn't keep it up. So I went to a gym to keep moving but it was a year later when my daughter and I restarted the 'couch to five kilometre' app. After all, we had managed to do it before but we got to week seven of nine and this time I encountered problems. We were running twenty five mins when I had a tight calf which I had to stop for and stretched out a couple of times during the run but as I ran on I heard and felt a sudden pop and felt an excruciating pain in my calf. I partially snapped my achilles tendon in my soleus muscle in my right calf. This stopped me in my tracks and resulted in four months sick leave from work. I had intense physio and ended up on crutches. I ended up having a year away from running due to the ongoing achilles and calf tenderness.

As I don't like to be beaten and I still have passion for running I'm currently running once again. I feel great as I feel the strength of my body as I run once again and as it releases my endorphins it makes me feel so alive.

As I run, I shut out the world and any negative feelings or behaviours I may have. For a while I can be nameless where no one knows me and take some relief from any symptoms. I use music to motivate me. I like Coldplay, Rock Anthems, especially from the eighties when I was a vibrant teenager. Led Zeppelin, Queen, Genesis, Prince or The Beatles are other favourites, such a good beat to exercise to. Bruce Springsteen reminds me of the days when I was driven to college by my elder brother. Sometimes I feel like a little dance will burst out of me as I'm so happy running, and I have the music so loud but then I quickly recall where I am.

The music I listen to in the car and whilst at the gym is more cheerful, the colours outside are often brighter to me and I feel a happiness inside once again.

CHAPTER TWENTY FOUR
ARE WE THERE YET?

I had fond memories of the 'Are we there yet?'- repeated questioning of all young travelling children. We said it as we slid around on those silky sleeping bags on the back seat of my dad's car. My children have asked it too. It became a game on a long car journey to amuse tiny precious minds with our different answers every time the same question was asked. Now it has a new meaning and thoughts connected to the saying. How do I know if I'm there yet if I don't know where I'm going? I have been so very lost.

My current answer is that I'm getting there. I can't always visualise what being well looks like. I have no idea what the future of my mental health holds.

I knew that I was damaged by this episode and the internal scars remain with me. I'd always hoped one day this episode would end; resulting in feeling as happy as I did before it all happened. But the sadness remains inside me although the rawness has healed. I don't think the scars will ever disappear.

I know the lack of support at work, prior to and during my illness contributed greatly to the severity and length of the depression. Initially, I was very angry towards the managers that failed to recognise the stress and sadness I was living with. I was honest and went to them numerous times before my sick leave and my difficulties were dismissed.

When I first returned to work, I couldn't make eye contact with this manager. I was still so very angry. The most anger I've felt towards one person. She confided in a co-worker who then explained for me (in my absence) about my difficult feelings towards her. This went on for six or eight weeks. I could see that I had to deal with the feelings or risk feelings of bitterness clinging to me and I recognised that this had the potential to limit my recovery. She came to me and sat with me while the investigation report was published and we read it together. She made her peace with me.

I made a decision to speak to another of the managers who failed me. I was listened to. She didn't even make a vague apology but explained that she had previously helped a co-worker too much. 'She'd become too involved and cared too much.' I didn't know who this colleague was, she'd cared for and I didn't care. It just sounded like an excuse. A strength came from within, 'I didn't see anyone from the establishment for months, during my eleven month sick leave. I'd been employed by the same place for eighteen years of my career. I was confused, severely depressed and belonged nowhere. That wasn't caring too much. I was at the lowest point of my life. I was suicidal and you didn't care.' Then I broke down and cried. The loneliness and fear connected to the illness still so very clear in my mind.

I think she knew she'd failed me. I had liked her but she failed me.

The meeting we had was perfectly timed. I was ready to say what I needed to say out loud and unknowingly it would be my last opportunity to have a discussion with her as she left to work elsewhere the next day. The acknowledgement meant I was able to cut myself free from the bitter negative feelings that had built up inside towards them. I didn't want negative feelings or any extra baggage to carry into my future. The scars are difficult and heavy enough to carry.

They just made mistakes. After all, who could have imagined the severity of my struggles that were to come? I knew myself better than anyone and I didn't see it coming. I actually took a long time to understand the complexity of the illness and how I could help and heal myself.

I know medically speaking, that I will be expected to become ill again due to my severe history. When I am stable with medication I can't see it. I also can't see it because the complexity of all the contributory factors couldn't all be presented to me in the same way again. But on low days, I think I won't have the strength or the staying power to live through another depressive episode and I feel panicked and fearful by this. Other days, I think if it does happen I have learned skills to truly persevere and keep myself safe until improvement would in time occur again.

I read books. I read other people's accounts of depression to see if they had answers that would help me. What I really needed was time, plenty of it. I needed to validate what were very difficult and tragic circumstances that I experienced. I needed time to process and comprehend my own actions building up to the breakdown and my reaction to it all. Finally, it was as if the illness had less energy to survive and it could no longer live within me. I stopped fearing depression returning I learned with my amazing counsellor to accept it for all it was. That indeed I always kept reaching out so this made me safe.

Once I was treated with a therapeutic combination of drugs the suicidal thoughts disappeared and I knew clearly in my mind I wouldn't do that to myself or to my family or friends. I felt once more that I was blessed to have the life I had. I'd been loved. I had three amazing daughters and an employer who now supported me and worked with me to ensure I was a safe and well worker. I did have special adjustments in place as I remained medicated at night so I no longer do shift work or night work and this definitely helped contribute to me staying stable.

I'm delighted to say I have had surprisingly good things happen to me in my working life. I applied for funding to take an 'innovative idea' forward shortly after my return to work. After all, I had nothing to lose by applying. I travelled to London to discuss a training bursary and was given two and a half thousand pounds after a successful interview to pay for a course and expenses to train at the Active Birthing Centre. It was with a pioneer, who supported women in their education of active birth and empowered them to believe in their own bodies to birth naturally. Her and her small team address and discuss options in a positive way if labour wasn't going to plan in their dynamic work. It was very positive and I was able to return to my clinical work and enhance the experience of the clients. I returned from the course with a buzz determination to plan and carry out this work.

One day, working on the labour ward I was looking after a lovely lady who had complications with her first labour. It was protracted and led to a forceps delivery which was a long way from what she had wished for. We talked of methods to enhance her second labour this time and I encouraged her to walk, stand and stay off the bed. I raised the bed so she could lean comfortably against it but not on it as she wanted to do everything to have a normal birth. She was tired but her labour was very brisk and she settled on a floor mat surrounded by cushions supported by her husband who sat behind her and cradled her on her haunches. The baby was delivered by me in a huge splash of amniotic fluid. I was covered; soaking. I used the towels that I had to dry the baby and handed him to his delighted mother. I rang the call bell for some more towels as I hadn't delivered the placenta so couldn't leave the room. My line manager arrived and couldn't see us behind the bed and her face was so surprised when I popped my head up from

behind the bed, to ask for towels. I reassured her that all was well and I continued with what I had to do. The parents were delighted by their straight forward delivery and once I was safe to do so I left them, comfortable in the bed, so I could change into scrubs and wash the liquor off my face!
It led my colleague who attended with me and supported me through the course to develop a more modern way to teach the women and their families in the community a positive parent craft course for her women. I was so busy prior to the illness that I wouldn't have even acknowledged the advertisement even for such a chance to obtain such a significant amount of funding.

After all that I had been through, I felt that it was important to speak honestly about what happened to me, and be transparent about my mental health. It was real and I needed to verbalise what happened to make sense of it. I hoped that in writing about my experience that the stigma would be reduced as some people would be educated about mental health conditions. I felt that I experienced this to develop my compassion with others even more and maybe to learn a life lesson. I thought I knew and understood mental health conditions but I certainly hadn't understood how badly it had an impact on every area of the sufferers life and those around them. I certainly understood after my experience.

Six years after the start of the illness I became a mental health champion and mental health first aider at work. My role enabled me to start conversations about mental health affecting colleagues or family members and clients alike. It also empowered me to be able to support and direct someone in a mental health crisis to seek help and prevent immediate harm to themselves. Ideally, I would like to be a voice which is heard; maybe in the form of some public speaking. This may not be easy for me initially as I do become nervous in this setting. Hopefully my passion to speak openly about my situation and to inform others of the importance of self care and compassion would help a lot of people in my personal and professional life. I can support people a lot especially when I have times experiencing a normal and not low mood. When my mood deteriorates I still lack self-esteem and self-belief which can be hard especially as my job is emotionally demanding as well as being quite physically tiring.

    I often connected to the MIND website for support of myself at times when I struggled with my moods and feelings. I have supported the 'Time to Talk' day by being present in the hospital café to start conversations about people's mental health. It was incredibly positive which maybe isn't the first thought people would have about talking about mental health. I engaged in a conversation with an older woman about mental health and she opened up to me once I explained I was a midwife. She told me the story of her birth some forty seven years before. In great detail, she explained she lacked support afterwards when she suffered postnatal depression. She explained her feelings of shame and isolation and how it affected her relationship negatively with her child up to the current time. I gave her a support number for counselling and suggested that it's never too late to talk to the child and explain the reasons for the difficult relationship. She said she would engage in counselling and talk to her adult child to make future improvements as a result. It was very moving.

It has been a painful illness but I believe in myself when my mood is steady and have the hope of a positive future. No one knows what life will bring to them but I am truly grateful for the good and positive situations that have presented themselves to me recently.

I'll always remember the pain of it all but I'll also remember that time is fluid and changeable and lessons can be learned from trauma and depression which eventually may shape and strengthen your future. I'm glad I truly persevered and engaged in the support services so I can now experience happiness and respect for all those that did help me.

I'm so grateful that my therapists worked so carefully with me and pushed the evil black dog well away. It was worth it. Once again many people are benefitting from me being around and I now appreciate and feel and enjoy the love in my heart that has been reawakened towards my lovely precious family and friends.

I'm truly grateful that I am in the second part of my life. I have developed a braveness which was not so apparent before as a result of persevering with the illness.

I can't describe the scarring that stays with me. It's as if a visible scar should be somewhere. I sometimes understood why some Europeans wear a black arm band during the grieving process. This is to make people aware of their loss and highlight pain that is felt. The scar is in my brain and deep deep in my heart. I know I'm scarred and yet others will forget or think I'm over it.

I'm still devastated for the family that the murder happened in, and the lost babies who were planned to come to our world but didn't reach it. I wanted to protect them all and I failed; through no fault of my own, but I feel I failed. A baby should not have been murdered on my watch.

CHAPTER TWENTY FIVE
SELF HELP AND SERVICE TO OTHERS

About eleven years ago I became a level two Reiki practitioner but rarely practised. I practised with willing family friends. Recently, when I was thinking of doing more self-help and self care, I thought of making my own small business practising Reiki. I find it very positive and very relaxing. I wondered why I hadn't thought of it sooner. The benefits of a compassionate Reiki service empowers my clients and also myself as I focus on the actual practice. I love meeting new clients and providing this service to support their own self care.

I feel that the pain I experienced gave me a unique insight into the minds of those who came to me with emotional issues, heartache or trauma. In the initial assessment of Reiki clients I was able to draw on the strength that allowed me to emerge on the other side of my experience. I then pass this strength and hope on to them. My business has been active for five years and been very successful and has a positive impact on my clients lives.
My clients were often still suffering from their own wounds and trauma. although some come
solely for relaxation. As I talked with them we built a professional relationship and I could offer empathy and relate closely to them. As I supported them I encouraged them to be heard and understood which I feel is vital in emotional upset.

Unlike the feeling of not being heard or understood by my managers in my situation.

Reiki is a gentle, powerful alternative, complementary therapy. Being compassionate, providing a service and watching clients successfully improve and recover increases my feelings of self worth and also of optimism. I'm happily using self Reiki and meditation as my tools to balance my energy and mind alongside my regular G.P. support.

I also used my compassionate attitude at work with the women I worked with. I encouraged conversations about perinatal mental health and made plans with them so they knew how to reach out for support if there was a deterioration in their mood antenatally or postnatally. I hoped that such conversations made talking about mental health less awkward or difficult for those I cared for. I also had many honest and open conversations with colleagues that I worked with so they can articulate their difficulties or concerns too and allow them to be truly heard and understood. I feel helping others with their mental health issues and being supportive is restorative and makes my own heart feel stronger.

I think my decision to be honest about my own mental health journey and reaching out to others shows that my pain didn't defeat me. Although it took over ten years to process what I experienced. At least I know I'm now moving into the future and the scars are less raw. I'm certain they will stay inside but my brain works more clearly when my mood is stable. I still feel there is improvement in my memory to be made. One day I may read a book and recall it easily instead of re-reading it to recall and comprehend it.

The braveness I feel since my recovery so far is a welcomed consequence and now I can make positive choices and experience normal emotions again.

I have seen my elder brother often for a walk in the lovely local park and we drank coffee and walked the new puppy, as sadly our beautiful white Bichon was ill and we had to say goodbye to him when he was only six years old. The new puppy came into our lives quite quickly as we couldn't pack the Bichon's toys and beds away; it was too final.

Our new dog is a Bichon cross and a very happy member of our family now. I was walking him at the local park one day and I bumped into a friend I had sadly lost touch with. I used to see her when we both walked our Bichons a couple of years before. It was so lovely to see her but when I looked she didn't have her Bichon either but a new dog. We had unknowingly lost our beloved dogs around the same time. We started to take the dogs to the park together and we became very good friends and so did our little dogs and when we get together it's always a perfect day. We enjoy time together walking or having wine or a meal. She is so upbeat and talkative. She is amazing to be with, we message each other everyday and meet when we can.

    I also reconnected with my lovely friend who I lost touch with when I was severely depressed. I was delighted. We walked at the park and had coffee every Sunday morning when I was not at work. If we did miss a couple of our park walks in a row we would meet after work for a drink and chat at the local bar and all seemed well with the world afterwards!

I sat with my dad when I could, so my Mam could have relief from being his carer every day and, like me, he slowly progressed. Step by tiny step. It seems to me, that whatever the complexities of any mental illness it's necessary to feel the pain, rest and then truly persevere and attend appointments for support. I believed that there was always someone to find to help you if you could engage with them. As I experienced, if the situation is complex it may take a few practitioners to support but recovery is always an option as long as you engage with the people that specialise in the area you need. The road to recovery may be long and turbulent but worth the battle in order to experience good days once again.

    I still struggle at times with a low or anxious mood but a recent counsellor made me realise that I always reach out when I've deteriorated which ensures my safety. She also highlighted how reaching out to others is not only courageous but shows healing is apparent.

CHAPTER TWENTY SIX
BEAUTY AND THE BEAST.

    I sat in the gynaecology clinic for my routine appointment after work. My usual consultant wasn't present but another that I had a good working relationship with. He sat my husband and I down. He told me why there were concerns with my symptoms and the situation they had been monitoring.

It was thought I had uterine cancer and samples couldn't be taken as this might seed the cancer elsewhere when it was disturbed. He said that I had to be referred to the regional gynaeoncologist for my case to be discussed at their regional multidisciplinary meeting that week to make a plan of action and decide where I would have an urgent abdominal hysterectomy and salpingo oophorectomy ie major abdominal surgery to remove all my reproductive organs. I was also referred for an MRI body scan within a two week time frame due to their concerns of possible other cancer sites.

    I was in shock as I wasn't expecting this information. I asked to wait for the procedure so I could process the information and continue improving my fitness but this was an urgent matter and I needed surgery as soon as possible. I felt I had no choice other than to sign the consent form for surgery before I left the appointment, dumbfounded at what I'd been told.

The consultant telephoned me after two days and said surgery would be in three weeks and the regional meeting had decided the operation should be straightforward so I could be dealt with in the local hospital. But the suspect tissue looked like a sarcoma and needed to be removed immediately.

I spoke to my line manager the very next day to explain my situation. She was as flabbergasted as I was and arranged for some leave for me to process the situation. She was incredibly supportive and she kept in close contact with me throughout the coming weeks.

My husband and mother were devastated as was I. My husband decided to decorate our bedroom so I could have a peaceful sanctuary to take time to rest and recuperate post operatively. There were no words really but my mind was in chaos.

What impact would this cancer have on my future health, my life and the lives of everyone in my family?

Will the surgery prevent further spread of the cancer?

We chose not to tell Dad as it was probably too much for him to deal with. He was upset enough that his only daughter, his baby girl, was to have major surgery.

The consultant then telephoned with my surgery date which was to be in three short weeks. He was attentive and supportive and vigilant with his plan of care for me and this was greatly appreciated. I spoke to my G.P. and received a fit note to support me in taking time away from my work. My thoughts were in turmoil and I was very upset that this was the situation when I had looked after my health all of my life. I suffered health anxiety as the information that the consultant had shared with me went round and round in my brain relentlessly. They think it's cancer. I was in disbelief that this was happening to me.

My girls, grown up now, were an amazing support as I shopped for everything I would need for my hospital stay and the following weeks as I recovered at home.

I didn't see what was to come next at all. My beloved dad suddenly collapsed as he suffered a massive brain haemorrhage. This time the bleed was over both hemispheres of his brain. He stood no chance of survival and died quickly in hospital. I had no time to say goodbye to him and that broke my heart.

I sobbed into my husband's arms on hearing the devastating news and the following days. My beloved Dad, my hero, was gone. I had to be the bravest I could be to support my mother who was now broken.

It was six days before my major surgery date. We had to decide a date for the funeral which was difficult in a large family with everyone's commitments. Unfortunately for me it was to be six days post surgery. I wanted a beautiful send off for my Dad and took charge of the plans and protected Mam best I could from conversations with the undertakers. I respected her wishes and we had organised everything we needed to in those five days before my surgery.

On the day of my surgery I was keen to have the cancer and all it entailed, removed.

Three days later I was discharged home and the fact that I'd hardly eaten as I had no appetite was overlooked. I hoped at home that I would manage the foods that I liked.

The next day I started vomiting and suffering abdominal distention and horrendous pain after eating. I was seen back at the hospital by a junior doctor and given a third antiemetic tablet to control the sickness. I struggled on like this for three days and wasn't tolerating any food so went to see my G.P. and I was told that it would settle down in time. I discussed how the nausea was present all of the time and the distention and vomiting caused me great distress but I was sent home. The day of Dad's funeral came and my daughters had to dress me and help me with my hair and make up. I was weak and in pain as the symptoms of the abdominal distention and vomiting persisted day and night. I prayed that I wouldn't vomit whilst I was saying goodbye to my beloved Dad. This would have devastated me as I already felt regret that I hadn't said goodbye to him at the hospital. I managed to stay at the funeral and it was a beautiful and fitting send off for a wonderful man that was so kind and helpful to so many people in his life.

As we left the service, I walked precariously with my husband through the crowds of people who all knew my Dad. I was so distressed as I hugged a few old friends but had to make a hasty exit to go back to the car and vomited once more. I was in no fit state to attend the wake and instead had to go home. This devastated me.

For another three days, ten days post operative, and I was still vomiting so I rang the gynaecological registrar that I worked with for help. I was unable to go to the same day urgent care center as I had initially as it was about to close for the evening. I waited five hours, vomiting in accident and emergency to seen. I was readmitted to the surgical ward and the next day I was told there were liver changes found in extreme vomiting and I attended an MRI scan which showed a partial bowel blockage as a result of the surgery but no other cancers. The consultant who told me of the concern I may have sarcoma had wanted to rule out other cancers in my body, so this was a relief. The general surgeon came and said I was not in need of surgery but that I would have to have water and intravenous therapy only to allow the bowel to rest and hopefully recover. I hadn't eaten for nine days and I was feeling very unwell and weak. It was a very lonely time in the sideroom of the ward. I cried frequently. My husband, girls and family visited for short times but the days were restless and long, unable to gain a comfortable post operative position on the bed or in the chair.

I was reviewed daily by my consultant colleagues and the surgeons and on the fourteenth day I was discharged home as I stopped vomiting and enjoyed some lemon cake - my Dads favourite.

On arriving home I was fragile as I had lost a lot of weight in the two weeks. I couldn't walk without holding on to something and I had to sit on a chair at the sink to freshen up and have support to shower from my husband or daughter.

The weeks went by and I felt very low and tearful so I saw a G.P. I didn't know this time if it was because I was grieving my Dad, having had major surgery or the lack of hormones. I soon improved when my hormones stabilized with hormone replacement therapy.

Dad was a huge miss over the coming weeks. I wanted to walk with him in the house and cut up his food as I did when I was with him. I wanted to go to the restaurant with him and buy him a beer. I wanted to dance with him once more as I had when I was a little girl and young adult. Neither of us had rhythm; we would start our dance with enthusiasm, Dad would twirl me around and we would dance a little but we were so hopeless at it we ended up sitting down embarrassed by our efforts. We giggled at our hopeless dance moves. He had a good sense of humour Dad but it was his kindness also that shone through in his life. He always supported me and had a good moral compass and was a good problem solver. I had waves of overwhelming emotion, missing my Dad daily and feeling scared of a life without him. My husband was a good support and my younger brother was so concerned about my health and kept in close contact with me.

Then some news that we had waited nine weeks for; the suspicious growth that was thought to be a sarcoma was negative for cancer.

I did not have cancer!?

This sent my mind into turmoil. I had processed the facts that had been given to me about having cancer that afternoon with the consultant. I was led to believe that I had cancer and now I was told that I didn't. This was obviously good news but it caused chaos in my mind. For nine weeks I thought of my life as a cancer sufferer and it took time to unravel these thoughts.

I had major surgery and was still recovering from it. It had a massive impact on my health, unable to exercise. I put the weight that I'd lost and more back on as a result of being sedentary. My cholesterol level increased rapidly leading to me worrying in case I was to succumb to a stroke like my father and his mother.

So I made dietary changes and lifestyle changes. I gradually recovered by walking and doing gentle yoga online but it was ten months before I could put on my running shoes and start the couch to five kilometre app. again. This time my trainer friend who I met at the gym was by my side in my recovery and to run with. Our friendship blossomed. I restarted circuit and pilates classes and was doing what I loved best once again.

Six months after Dads death and Mam was admitted to hospital for elective keyhole surgery with an expected hospital stay of three days. Her surgery was straight forward but unfortunately over the next nine weeks she was to suffer every complication possible. I was very concerned about her and visited with her every single day.

Initially she was in extreme pain post operatively. It was hard to know if this was from the gas inserted into the abdomen to visualise the area for surgery. She was immobile because of the uncontrolled pain and suffered multiple pulmonary embolisms. Then it was found bile was leaking into her abdomen, acting like a detergent, it caused sepsis and it eroded a liver artery. I was on my way to the hospital and I received a call to say that she was bleeding and that I should come in to see her immediately. On my arrival I found a nurse and she told me that Mam was in intensive care due to a ha emorrhage. On arrival at ITU, I was told by the receptionist to wait in the quiet room until staff were able to update me.

I broke down in tears. The pain of losing Dad alongside Mams health which was now in jeopardy, this was too much for me to cope with. The pain in my stomach was intense. I couldn't cope with losing Mam as well as Dad. The fear of this happening encompassed my whole being.

As I waited, I rang my brothers and they were both busy and they would wait for an update. I rang my good friend from work who had supported me throughout what had been an appalling year. The worst year since the acute onset of trauma and depression twelve years earlier. She was so sensible and grounded me as we waited for the all important update. I waited three hours in the quiet room until one of my brothers arrived. A nurse had come to inform me that Mam was having a procedure to stem the bleeding in another department but that's all I could tell him. I felt better with my younger brother by my side and we became very close during Mams hospital stay. He was actually my rock during this time.

Time blurred as we waited with numerous cups of tea and eventually we were shown into the intensive care unit to see Mam. She was in bed with so many machines alarming around her. She had a blood transfusion running and intravenous therapy. The procedure was successful and little did we know a further bleed would happen two days later and the procedure would need to be repeated. Unfortunately, the fluid and seven blood infusions caused Mam's weight to increase suddenly by twenty kilos. This then affected her lungs and heart and the ITU consultant came to tell my brother and I that if the heart was severely affected she may not survive. We gasped as we heard this news and I took my brother to the quiet room to discuss the situation that was unfolding in front of us. It was so stressful. I also wanted to give him space and privacy away from Mam and so I could support him and explain things as he admitted he didn't understand medical terms. I couldn't believe when Mam had a heart attack one morning. Her body was obviously under so much strain. Her life was at risk and we were extremely concerned but once again she fought through it.

After many procedures and weeks of antibiotics Mam was discharged still with signs of sepsis. Community nurses came to administer the intravenous antibiotics and one was a nurse I had trained with some thirty seven years earlier. I was astounded when he immediately recognised me and he was a great support to me over the coming weeks. I stayed with her at her home to help transition to life back at home. She was very weak after losing muscle mass during her hospital stay. Eventually she became stronger and I saw her strength of character coming back and she motivated herself to exercise so we could plan a cruise, just her and I. Just as we had months after Dad died. We wanted to rest and recuperate from my cancer scare and Dads death and Mam's hospital stay.

Astonishingly, my mood didn't lower apart from the initial response to my operation and I suddenly realised there was a light in my dark tunnel of my recent years of PTSD,anxiety and depression. During Mams hospital stay there were times that I was so worried she would die and this caused great pain within my heart so over a few months I re-evaluated my priorities and my life. A new G.P. has supported me through the difficult times over the last year. She followed me up every couple of weeks and I find her support phenomenal and also empowers me to make joint decisions to any medication changes with her. It also helps me cope knowing I can connect with her soon at the next appointment or contact her sooner if my thoughts/feelings or low mood become very difficult to cope with.

    Whilst Mam was in hospital I decided to retire from the NHS and saw my pension as a gift to enable me to leave. I wanted to support mam in rebuilding her life without Dad and finally focus on my emotional and physical health and spend time with my now adult daughters and their partners. I felt after thirty seven years in the NHS I had served sufficient time to leave it behind. The pressures, the highs and the lows. Literally the blood, sweat and tears. It meant no more 6am starts, Christmas day shifts but mainly no pressures from the workload and of time. It wasn't any easy decision but I tried to believe my path in life could only get better and once I transitioned that I would settle into retirement with my husband.

    I planned to fill my days with coffee dates, holidays, exercise and I started meditation regularly to bring joy and happiness to me. My Reiki business naturally progressed and I gained a lot more regular clients which brought me happiness. Even though I retired, it's not the end. I feel it is a new beginning. Life without Dad and life without my identity as a midwife. I believe in the continuous existence of the human soul and believe Dad continues to love and support me from afar, wherever that may be. This has greatly helped me in coping with his sudden death. I talk to him as if he's close and with me often I just won't tell the psychiatrist this!

My new goals are to focus on more self compassion and resist the difficult moods less as this may make the episodes persist. I'm also working on being kind to myself when the mood becomes low and overcoming the inner critic which has a harsh and negative voice. I need to treat myself as good as I treat others in order to minimize negative thoughts during difficult episodes. I have realised the importance and benefits of self care and have incorporated this into my life and I have become more resilient as a result.

I believe I can build a beautiful life for myself even though I lost many years of it to darkness and a wound that wouldn't close. I don't think that the healing process truly ends but I have realised the wounds don't stop me from being the person I want to be. Self care and exercise are a major part of my life now. I owe it to myself to be happy again and fall in love with life again.

I'm quite readily embracing my future and making it the best I can for all those special people in my life. I feel lucky to have the friends I have, new and old. My committed husband, my great brothers, mother and family who keep in touch with me. I'm so glad I'm moving on and grateful for the people I've met on my journey which is ongoing but full of hope and possibilities.

'And I just got broken
Broken in two
Still I call it magic
when I'm next to you…

And if you were to ask me, After
all that we've been through, Still
believe in magic?
Oh yes I do.'

Magic-Coldplay.2014.

And you ask 'What if I fall?'
'Oh but my darling what if you fly?'

Erin Hanson.2016.

Bibliography:

Institute of health metrics and evaluation. Global health data exchange.W.H.O (accessed 2023)

J.Cerel et al 2014 - Exposure to suicide and identification as survivor:Results from a random-digital survey.

chaosthroughtrauma_D.Goode@yahoo.com

Printed in Dunstable, United Kingdom